PRAISE FOR *THE CRUCIBLE'S GIFT*

"*The Crucible's Gift* offers leaders insight into their deepest places that define them. Prepare for a remarkable journey of self-discovery, guided by the stories of leaders who had the courage to go on record in this book and the insights of the author, James Kelley, whose own story made this book complete."

DR. MARSHALL GOLDSMITH, Thinkers50 #1 Leadership Thinker in the World

"James Kelley's extraordinary book, *The Crucible's Gift*, will guide you on a deep exploration of how to become an authentic leader—learning and growing from your crucible experience with increased self-awareness, integrity, compassion and ability to relate to others. Following Kelley's great wisdom will not only enable you to become a better leader but a better human being as well."

BILL GEORGE, senior fellow at Harvard Business School, former chair & CEO of Medtronic and author of *Discover Your True North*

"We all face challenges. James Kelley's insightful new book shows us how we can leverage adversity to become better leaders—and humans—by embracing our true selves."

DORIE CLARK, author of *Stand Out* and *Reinventing You* and adjunct professor at Duke University's Fuqua School of Business

"Everyone faces adversity and we all arrive at crucibles that dictate our next path. In this book, Dr. James Kelley highlights the 5 lessons we need to learn to succeed and how the 'micro-moments' we encounter help us become better leaders."

JEFFREY HAYZLETT, primetime TV & podcast host, speaker, author and part-time cowboy

"James Kelley shows us that adversity is part of anything built well."

BERNIE SWAIN, founder of Washington Speakers Bureau

"We all face moments of truth in life. How we handle these crucible moments ultimately define who we are. *The Crucible's Gift* is a powerful, insight-packed must-read. Dr. Kelley has given us the gift of an authentic look into what it really takes to design a legendary life."

CHRIS LOCHHEAD, host of *Legends & Losers* podcast, co-author of "instant classic" *Play Bigger: How Pirates, Dreamers, and Innovators Create and Dominate Markets*

"James Kelley brings characteristic enthusiasm and curiosity to this fascinating exploration of what helps leaders to succeed and thrive in today's challenging environment."

HAL MOVIUS, president of Movius Consulting

"We all have different strengths, but I can tell you that being authentic and humble hopefully are your dominant strengths. These are the ones that will take you to the next level in your personal and business life. I have learned a lot about myself, both strengths and weaknesses, but *The Crucible's Gift* taught me even more about myself and how I could still become an even better husband, father, grandfather and business leader and hopefully leave a legacy that I can be proud of. Study James Kelley's book. You will learn a lot more about yourself and about the people around you. It's never too late to get better. It's hard, but when you do the hard things life gets easier."

LEE COCKERELL, former executive vice president, Walt Disney World Resort and bestselling author of four books on leadership, management, customer service and keeping your career on track

"James Kelley interviews 140 leaders from all walks of life . . . in a compelling and compassionate manner with a delightful and irreverent self-dialogue. This is an inspiring piece of work. This will bring up your self-awareness of your own qualities of leadership and give a clear focus on how to be a better version of yourself."

DENNIS BOYLE, co-founder and partner of IDEO

"The impact of toxic leadership is well documented, yet organizations still fall victim to a lack of integrity and honesty at the top. *The Crucible's Gift* opens up an important conversation about the stuff authentic leaders are made of—and you will meet many in this book whose stories are benchmarks for all of us. Highly recommended."

JON BERGHOFF, president of Flourishing Leadership Institute and creator of the LEAF Certification

THE CRUCIBLE'S GIFT

DR. JAMES KELLEY

FOREWORD BY **Joe Burton**

THE

CRUCIBLE'S GIFT

5 LESSONS FROM AUTHENTIC LEADERS

WHO THRIVE IN ADVERSITY

Executives
AFTER HOURS

Executives After Hours
16408 NE 13th Street
Vancouver, WA
98684 USA
www.drjameskelley.com

978-0-9998915-1-3 (paperback)
978-0-9998915-0-6 (ebook)

Every reasonable effort has been made to contact the
copyright holders for work reproduced in this book.

Produced by Page Two
www.pagetwostrategies.com
Cover design by Taysia Louie
Interior design by Peter Cocking

18 19 20 21 22 5 4 3 2 1

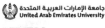

جامعة الإمارات العربية المتحدة
United Arab Emirates University

UAEU

To my dad, I miss you, and I know you are proud of me.

———————————————

Don't let fear conquer you—conquer your fear.

CONTENTS

FOREWORD

I MET DR. James Kelley through a mutual friend who had previously appeared on James's award-winning podcast, *Executives After Hours*. At the time, I had no idea that his work would become a constant source of new ideas, inspiration and challenges for me to personally grow as a leader.

James's work, education and personal story of struggling with early loss and inner demons make him uniquely qualified to write about authentic leadership and adversity. Beyond being on his own journey, he's tapped into insights from more than 140 of the world's top leaders. His podcast has helped professionals around the world to reflect, cultivate a sense of purpose and reconnect to their authentic self.

The book has many insightful moments, but the one that holds the most truth for me is "the obstacle is the path." That line epitomizes James's desire to speak with well-respected leaders who share their bumpy roads to success. He approaches the storytelling with humor, irreverence, warmth and the desire to help each of us build momentum as we take on those obstacles. With *The Crucible's Gift*, James provides the personal stories, insights and mindset for success that is so often born from the challenges that begin early in life.

The first time I met James, he said, "I care about who you are, not what you do, because who you are defines what you do." It's that caring that allows him to share the unique insights to help any leader to cultivate a strong foundation built on purpose, self-awareness, integrity, compassion, relatableness and a commitment to lifelong learning. Here, you'll find tools to help crawl, walk and climb the road to success without losing yourself.

Authentic leadership and adversity is a timely topic. Technology is changing every aspect of how leaders think, work, collaborate and the very nature of what "success" means. What you know today will largely be stale, out of date and increasingly irrelevant in the next ten years. At the same time, the pace of modern business and related stress that comes from facing constant change and disruption is slowly turning many leaders into the worst version of themselves: commanding, overwhelmed and distracted.

If you're concerned about your own well-being and performance in the face of adversity, you are not alone. Stress takes a $550 billion toll on U.S. businesses every year in the form of absenteeism, lost productivity and healthcare costs. The Gallup Organization reports less than 31 percent of U.S. and Canadian employees are "engaged" at work and less than 17 percent globally. The Edelman Trust Barometer reports a "crisis in trust" with the largest-ever drop reported across all major institutions in 2017. Specifically, a minority of people now trust the Media (43 percent), Government (41 percent), CEOs (37 percent) and Political leaders (29 percent).

Study after study confirms that business has a problem. Four key employee themes are emerging: a sense of injustice, lack of hope, lack of confidence and a desire for change. Employees around the world overwhelmingly now find other employees to be more credible than their own senior management or CEOs.

There's a clear movement towards employees wanting leaders to speak with them, not at them. They prefer spontaneous to rehearsed, blunt to diplomatic and personal experience over data. Employees want to be themselves. They want transparency. They want truth. They're feeling the pressure themselves. And they are demanding authenticity.

James defines a "crucible" as "a significant moment, positive or negative impact, which forces a leader to become introspective... assess their strengths and weaknesses, leading them to become more self aware." From this moment comes clarity, happiness and growth.

My crucible moment came from a culmination of a 20-plus year career as a global COO in high stress, high performance Fortune 500 companies. After a rough start, growing up in a home plagued by alcohol and drug abuse, I was travelling the world, working around the clock, and making more money than I'd ever imagined. Like so many professionals, decades of high stress took a toll on my physical health and mental well-being, and ultimately, my performance. Instead of being elated with success, I was a stressed out, deeply unhappy workaholic, in constant pain and missing out on my life. I hadn't just hit a wall; I'd turned into a different person. It impacted my performance to the point where I was basically being paid to fly around the world to stress people out. Try putting that on a business card.

My crucible came in the form of a health crisis. It happened in my early forties, driven by stress, two herniated discs, insomnia, the loss of two siblings, one to a heart attack and the other to suicide, and a wife who cared more about my well-being than I did myself.

My reflection led me to start a mindfulness meditation practice to help manage my own stress, insomnia and pain. That resulted in me stepping away from a successful career running global ad agency networks to help other professionals reduce stress and increase their resilience. Today my company, Whil, is the world's leading digital well-being training company. We work with 120+ companies around the world, helping millions of professionals to live healthier, happier and more engaged lives.

Unless you have some touchstone to measure yourself against, it's hard to compare the leader that you aspire to be to the person you've become. It can be hard to align your public and private self. It can be easy to buy into the fallacy of charm. The migration to a foreign, more angry Joe wasn't evident to me. On the contrary, I had tremendous success while being impatient, angry and competitive. I racked up promotions, stock, bonuses and plenty of congratulatory steak dinners. My approach worked. Until it didn't.

James's work has helped me to realize that living in the age of disruption means that we professionals constantly have to reinvent ourselves. The future requires focus, resilience and a growth mindset. If you're not on a path to cultivate a positive, curious, collaborative and nonjudgmental leadership style, now is the time to get started.

With *The Crucible's Gift*, James has delivered leaders not only the touchstone, but a trusted board of advisors. You'll hear from friends and leaders like Chris Boyce, Bill George and Laura Putnam. You'll gain insights from companies as diverse as Google, IDEO and the NHL. You'll practice techniques to reverse the mind's natural tendencies towards negativity. You'll tap into reflection as an ongoing source of truth and inspiration. Simply put, you'll learn from the experiences of high-performing leaders with grit.

The stories, crucible moments and practices presented provide a unique opportunity. So many of the leaders here faced tremendous odds, traumas and setbacks to experience their own crucible and use that to set a true north. James has given us each the opportunity to pause and reflect. You don't have to wait until you hit a wall to discover your own crucible.

The challenges facing leaders across industries, geography and cultures are shockingly similar. If you feel like you're experiencing life at the rate of several WTFs per hour, you're not alone. It doesn't matter what line of work you're in. There is a universal truth: adversity is the norm. It's getting harder to manage the pace of modern business and the related impact that stress is having on our lives.

The Crucible's Gift is a call to action to thrive in adversity to be the authentic leader that your team, company and family needs; driven to do right, both professionally and personally.

About Joe Burton

JOE BURTON is the founder and CEO of Whil Concepts, the leading digital well-being training platform helping employees to reduce stress, increase resilience and improve their sleep and performance. He's an entrepreneur in scientific well-being, former president of Headspace and spent fifteen years as a global COO in public companies. Joe is an alumnus of Harvard Business School, author of *Creating Mindful Leaders* and regular contributor to *Forbes, Business Insider* and the *Huffington Post.* He's worked in over fifty countries and travels the world speaking on disruption, resilience, culture, emotional intelligence and mindfulness as a competitive advantage. Joe is also a certified *Search Inside Yourself* instructor. Find out more at whil.com.

INTRODUCTION

THE IMPORTANCE OF
BEING GENUINE

THERE ARE ONLY two certainties in life: change and death. Let's start a leadership book by talking about death, shall we? Seems metaphorically appropriate.

Consider how many of us will go through this life, working for 40-plus years, just plodding along. Some will advance to the highest levels in a chosen career, while others will be happy just to collect a paycheck to pay the bills. Fast-forward to the twilight of our professional career, and at the ripe old age of 65 or 70, we retire and hope we worked long enough to live comfortably. Maybe we'll find a hobby, spend time with grandkids, see the world. At the end of our journey we will, yes, die. Death is inevitable.

Let's say on average you work for 45 years, for 48 weeks a year, and for 40 hours a week. That means you spent 86,400 hours at work. Now, if that doesn't slightly depress you, consider that many of us live to work and not the other way around. The majority of us will spend 86,400 hours of our life being *not* our best self, but rather a lesser version of our best self. And thus, at the end of 45 years, 48 weeks a year, 40 hours a week, we spent 86,400 hours slowly dying by a thousand paper cuts.

Let me tell you a story about Joe Burton, CEO of Whil Concepts, Inc. Joe should have died by age 50 (he's not quite there yet). In his early forties, Joe made a choice.

Whil Concepts offers digital well-being training programs to help people live healthier, happier, more engaged lives. Joe and I met for my *Executives After Hours* podcast to talk about his personal journey. Prior to this role, at only 40, Joe was chief operating officer (COO) at McCann Worldgroup (an Interpublic Group company) and head of the Microsoft global business, a position he held from 2006 to 2009. Many people in the advertising industry would kill to be at that level at that age. But Joe decided to step down. When he advised the CEO of his decision, the CEO said, "Are you crazy? You're in a job that you can coast through and retire. That's the job you've got. You're insane." Joe's reply was, "I'm going to go start my own business. I want to do something that matters." The CEO's response was lacking in subtlety: "You're an idiot."

Looking through the CEO's lens, Joe *was* an idiot for quitting, and at some level Joe may have agreed, but what the CEO didn't fully appreciate is that for nearly forty years the air around Joe had been slowly sucked up by drama, and he was suffocating. As Joe says, "I'm running the global Microsoft business; we've got fifty thousand employees around the world. I'm basically flying around the world stressing people out, showing up, telling employees to be faster, cheaper, let's get this done, let's hit the numbers, let's win!" It was this mentality that catapulted Joe to COO.

However, in the race to the top, Joe's competitive drive was compounded by his fair share of personal challenges, and with each challenge Joe's sense of true north began to shift and his focus was redirected inward. Over a two-year period, Joe lost his older sister to a heart attack and his twin sister took her own life after decades of addiction. His father died twelve years earlier. Adding to the personal challenges, Joe's body and mind were beginning to break down. It was almost like a snake eating its tail: the higher Joe rose in the organization, the more he traveled, the less time he devoted to keeping fit, and the more weight he gained. All of this resulted in two herniated discs, insomnia and asthma. Sounds pretty awesome, doesn't it?

A by-product of Joe's drive to climb to the top of the mountain by 40 is that Joe lost Joe. He didn't know who Joe was. His body didn't know who Joe was. And Joe's mind—well, I think Joe could probably tell you better... it got lost on its own journey as well. Joe was a stranger to his authentic self. As Joe was losing Joe, a doctor suggested he try meditation. At 40 Joe felt that this was "hippie-dippie" stuff. Furthermore, he was sure that he would get laughed out of the boardroom if they found out he was practicing mindfulness. As happens in life, the nudges were piling up and Joe was falling down. Fast-forward to age 43 and Joe came to the realization that a course correction was needed. He wanted to find himself, reengage with his family, repair his mind and body. He began a mindfulness practice.

What Joe found is that by spending ten to fifteen minutes a day on mindfulness training, he was able to recalibrate his core self and begin a journey of personal transformation, find his new true north. During this journey, Joe's competitive drive for external validation of his success was swapped for a deeper understanding of himself, a more meaningful relationship with his family, and clarity around his relationship with his father. To Joe, this was his awakening, and from it was born Whil.com.

When you listen to the full podcast interview of Joe's journey (episode 76), what stands out the most is his passion for what he is doing now. Whil is a direct reflection of Joe's desire to share his transformation with a larger corporate audience. I think the largest takeaway from his story is the role of all life's nudges in taking him to a point where he made a life-altering decision—to change direction by leaving the advertising industry behind in a moment of, in some people's eyes, insanity.

Many of us set out on a particular career path in our early twenties because we want to achieve something great. However, we don't know what "great" means. We typically think "great" is associated with making wads of money and having an impressive title and trophies on the mantel. But this runs contrary to Joe's story. Joe had "greatness," if you define it in terms of money and recognition. But he was running from his childhood and from his environment in Pittsburgh. He wanted to be something different, and I admire and respect him because I often feel the same way.

What's ironic about life, whether we like it or not, is eloquently stated by Mo Gawdat, the former chief business officer for Google X, in his 2017 book *Solve for Happy*. One of Mo's core beliefs is that life will give us nudges to move us in the direction we are meant to travel. And when you resist going in that direction, Mo says (and I am paraphrasing), life will kick you in the face and knock your teeth out. This is what happened to Joe: his teeth metaphorically got kicked out. His back was shot, two of his sisters had passed away, his dad had passed away and, I think he would agree, he was slowly killing himself. Fifty was looking like a bleak landscape.

Over the course of a meteoric career, Joe got lost in the sea of success and was left searching for his authentic self. He knew his authentic self was there, deep down inside—and I mean *deep*. Like many who have come before him, and many who will come after, Joe found out that the view from the mountaintop is not all it is cracked up to be. He realized that he needed more of what life was capable of giving, and in his case that realization came in the form of a spiritual awakening, one that led to an understanding of the need for compassion: compassion for those around him, compassion for his wife and, most importantly, compassion for Joe.

As I took notes on my interview with Joe to prepare for this book, I found myself reflecting on the fact that many of us do a job because we think that's what we're "supposed" to do, not because it's what we *want* to do. Many of us lack the will to pursue our passions, for any number of reasons. One reason may be our parents' voices echoing in our head, telling us to be a lawyer, doctor or accountant, and not a philosopher, musician or rocket scientist.

When I was an assistant professor at a private university in the U.S., students would come to my office and share the pressure their parents put on them to pick the job that would make the most money. They rarely said, "I wish my parents would stop telling me to follow my passion." They sat across from me, a tissue in hand, and I could see the agony on their faces as they tried to balance their parents' wishes with their own desires. I found myself overwhelmed with compassion for them, and often counseled them to screw their parents and follow their passion, aiming to nudge them onto that path. As Joe's tale points out, success at the top is rarely as glorious as it seems. The Notorious B.I.G. said it best: "Mo Money Mo Problems."

As a dad of four, I know that the paternal pressure to make sure my children succeed in life (whatever that means) is real. That pressure is particularly palpable in the U.S., where many parents want to get their kids into the best private schools, have them take music lessons and play on the best sports teams. How many languages does your kid know? And it's all in the name of getting their child into the best universities. I would never fault a parent for those desires, and I fight the temptation. Yet I fall for it all at the same time. These expectations can produce a culture of impressing others with titles and positions ... and a deficit of personal happiness. For most of us, this is how the long journey to inauthentic living starts.

What do Joe Burton's story and my brief parental discussion have to do with authentic leadership? Everything! We bestow a false glorification of happiness and authenticity onto our children in the hope of providing them with the foundations for "success," but it's hollow. Why? Because we provide them with false narratives about happiness and authenticity. Who wouldn't get lost on such a journey?

Why and How I Came to Write About Authentic Leadership

I would love to share some meaningful story about my journey to this book, but I don't have one. The topic found *me*. When I arrived in Australia to pursue my PhD, I asked myself what I wanted to accomplish over the next ten years. As I stared at a blank page, I began to see myself at 43. I didn't see four kids and three continents later, but what I did write down was that I wanted to complete a book. So, with that goal sitting somewhere in the back of my mind, in 2015 I began *Brave Endurance Wellness Podcast*. The aim was to learn as much as I could about the corporate wellness space by interviewing industry leaders. Over the next seventy or so interviews, I wanted to get a better understanding of the messy concept of wellness, so I asked every wellness leader how *they* defined wellness. This was going to be the crux of the book: *The Wellness CEO*.

However, at about interview number 50, something started whispering in my ear. Now, if you haven't listened to a podcast, shame on you. Go to iTunes, search for *Executives After Hours* and subscribe. Have a listen to one of the 140-plus interviews. I will wait . . .

So now that you have listened to a podcast or three, you know that I take the listener on a journey from my guest's childhood through the present day. My tagline is "I care about who you are, not what you do, because who you are defines what you do." At episode 70 of *Brave Endurance*, the themes I had noticed emerging by episode 50 kept making an appearance, and that had me curious and excited. I became intrigued about *all* leaders, not just leaders in the wellness space. I decided to change the title of the podcast to *Executives After Hours* to explore some new directions, and a book on authentic leadership was born.

To gain a deeper understanding of authentic leadership, I talked to leaders across a plethora of industries: health and wellness, finance, marketing, hospitality and resorts, publishing (authors like Bill George, authentic leadership expert), entrepreneurship, tech, consulting, sustainability and more. The executives and other leaders came from more than 140 different companies. This book is not a compilation of quotes, but rather a series of excerpts from interviews that tell the guests' stories as we explore this phenomenon called authentic leadership.

As a researcher, you learn that there are two types of research: inductive and deductive. Inductive research occurs when a researcher investigates seemingly random bits of information looking for patterns that inform new and unique ideas. Deductive research is a systematic process in which a researcher starts with a conclusion based on multiple premises that are generally assumed to be true. For this book, I used an inductive approach, starting with a clean slate and developing a model that I then explore. I will unpack it in a few paragraphs.

But first, let's return to the workplace theme. On average a person spends about 40 hours a week at work. You spend more "awake" time at the office than you do at home. So the question I often ask is, "Wouldn't you want to work someplace where the leader will accept nothing less than an environment that allows employees to be themselves—and their *better* selves—for those 40-plus hours a week?" More importantly, wouldn't you want to be that leader who *creates* the environment for others to be their authentic selves? I hope that this book provides a new perspective on being who you are or can be as a leader, which is as important as who you are as a parent, grandparent, partner or friend. Now, I am sure some of you may be thinking, "Yeah, what type of utopian world does *this* guy live in?" To these opinions I say, fair critique. But what if the proposition put forth suggests that being your authentic self and creating an authentically led organization actually increases the bottom line? What would you think then? Stay tuned.

Finally, I have intentionally avoided defining *authentic leadership* although I do suggest several factors that have what I believe to be a significant impact on one's authentic self. At the end, you will arrive at your own conclusions about leading authentically. The book is meant to be a process of discovery. Every process needs a starting point, so here is a brief overview.

Foundations of the Authentic Leadership Model

Academic researchers discuss authentic leaders as having four main attributes: self-awareness, relational transparency, balanced processing and internalized moral perspective.

Self-awareness is present when the leader is aware of how they process information and come to understand the world. They understand their strengths and weaknesses. *Relational transparency* is present when the leader is authentic in their interactions with those around them. They are honest and present their true self, while keeping that presentation appropriate (that is, within bounds). They engage in *balanced processing*: maintaining an objective perspective and looking at all relevant information before making a decision. The final aspect is the *internalized moral perspective*. The leader acts according to their moral standards and will not corrupt them despite external pressures or fear of consequences.

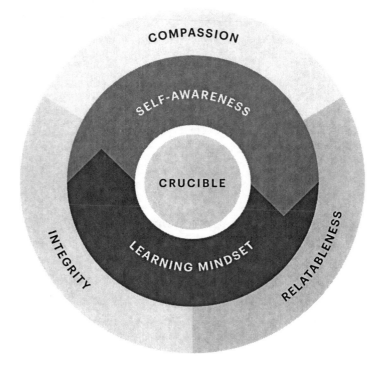

AUTHENTIC LEADERSHIP MODEL

This book goes beyond the literature to discuss three more concepts that I believe have a significant impact on a leader's authentic self. First, similar to concepts put forth by the late Dr. Warren Bennis, the distinguished leadership professor at the University of Southern California, a leader's personal or professional crucible is at the center of their personal or professional growth. Second, borrowing from Carol Dweck's work on growth mindset, I discuss the support of learning for an individual's growth. Finally, mixed in all of this and at the same level of relatableness (relational transparency) and integrity (moral perspective), is the impact of compassion on a leader's ability to create moments that relieve colleagues' suffering.

As I started to build the framework for the book, a clear order of cause and effect emerged, along with a model of authentic leadership. The model consists of three layers that interact with one another depending on the leader's crucible—the stage of personal and professional growth—and mindset.

At the center of the Authentic Leadership Model is the crucible, which is discussed in chapter 1. The crucible is a significant moment, positive or negative in impact, which forces a leader to become introspective. It also creates an opportunity for an individual to assess their strengths and weaknesses, leading them to become more self-aware. Lisa McDonald, a former Canadian television personality and author of children's illustrated books with a twenty-five-year history in social work, provides an example. Here's what she has to say about her crucible:

When we initially spoke, James, behind the scenes quite some time ago, you would know that I don't believe in coincidences. I really believe that oftentimes our darkest periods within our own lives, our own experiences, pretty much [dictate] the path that we feel that we're intended to be on, and so as a result of some unfortunate things that happened in my childhood—namely, abuse, sexual abuse—I always felt naturally drawn to people who are going through difficult times. As I learned to empower myself, find my voice and stand up for myself, I began to make good choices along the way.

Not always, but always aspiring to do so, and being very committed to my own growth and evolution of self, I just naturally fell upon the line of work that allowed me to advocate for other people. To help other people empower themselves. To find their own voices, as you never know what life is going to throw at you, and I believe that a lot of it comes down to choice. We can wallow in self-pity, we can become victims in our life or we can take the unfortunate things that have happened to us and find the lesson, find the gift. (Episode 102)

Lisa's crucible allowed her to take stock of her life, appreciate her journey and embrace her professional and personal growth. Stated another way, Lisa used her self-awareness to instigate changes.

In chapter 2 we tackle the impact of self-awareness on our ability to grow and strengthen our professional and personal self and connect the process of increasing one's self-awareness to crucibles.

John Toomey is an Australian known around the world as a fatigue prevention expert, author of the *Life Wisdom Newsletter* and a *Huffington Post* contributor. John and I discussed the overwhelming impact a personal development course called Avatar had on his self-awareness and growth:

I had an amazing experience with my dad giving me this brutal belting. For years, because he was a big guy, my dad, I had this charge on my dad being a bully. I wasn't even looking at this [when] I was looking at something else, [a situation] that comes up repeatedly in my life, and I was exploring it. You're not exploring it through thinking or analysis; you're feeling your way into it. I landed in that situation and I went, "Oh God, *this* is where that comes from." Then as I explored it, I went, "Oh, *that's* what I did to my dad just before that happened."

It was like I could see how my dad, what he did was in response to something I did—those sorts of things. When you're doing the [Avatar] course, it's your own exploration. Nobody's telling you what you've got to find or what you should find, because nobody else knows. (Episode 56)

Next, the Authentic Leadership Model suggests that heightened self-awareness leads to integrity, compassion and relatableness.

In chapter 3, I present the concept of integrity as a key attribute of an authentic leader. I break down the moral integrity and behavioral impact they have in a leader-follower relationship.

In chapter 4, compassion is discussed as a tool authentic leaders use to create shared meaning with their colleagues, and also as a process for leaders' own personal development. Additionally, I make the business case as to why compassion can help the bottom line of the organization. Across my interviews, I found many leaders who are authentic and compassionate. They were eager to relieve the suffering, big or small, of others around them. They shared stories of sadness and stories of how happiness provided them an opportunity to gain a unique perspective on others' lives.

Jay Scott, co-director of Alex's Lemonade Stand Foundation, was galvanized by the death of his daughter, Alex, to work to relieve the suffering of others. He told me why he does this work:

So, the easiest thing would have been for us [Jay and his wife, Liz] to just walk away and move on with our life. But we talked, and we decided that, you know what? We could help a lot of people, a lot of kids, if we keep what Alex started going. The downside of that was we were going to have to relive things over and over and over again. So, if you talked to me ten years ago and said, "Did you make the right decision?" I would say I'm not sure, but if you ask me now, I'd say, "Yes, we made the right decision. It's not about us; it's about the kids." We've gotten over a lot of the difficulty in retelling the story. (Episode 44)

In chapter 5 we look at the final aspect of the impact self-awareness has on relatableness, a core attribute of authentic leadership. I think *relatableness* is a made-up word, because there's always a red squiggly line under it when I type it. But it makes the point I want to make. Leaders in my interviews who identified that they had a crucible—one that led to the realization of compassion—were able to create shared meaning with people across their organization. I found that relatable leaders actively seek out people across their organization to learn more about them as individuals. They realize that making a personal connection creates a moment that can impact that person's life, whether it's for the day, for the week, or for the month. I found these people amazing to talk to—they seemed to have the ability to be present, to listen and to be insightful. For example, Elise Carr, MA, sexuality expert (yes, and a leader) and former model, discusses her favorite threesome (head out of the gutter, please):

That's why I often speak about my favorite threesome, as I term it, and I've written an article on this. It's about the three relationships you should always be in. The first one is with yourself. I call this your soul, and you need to nourish that in some small way every single day, like it's a nonnegotiable, even if it's five minutes with your cup of tea in the morning, you know? Whatever it is that nourishes you before you get going.

And then you move on to your second relationship, which is with spirit, god, goddess, divine, universe, Buddha... whatever you want to call that higher power. Sometimes people refer to it as their higher self—whatever resonates with you. Having a connection—let's just call it spiritual connection—having a spiritual connection every day, whether that's going to church, sitting on the yoga mat, being under a tree, connecting in some capacity and opening yourself up for some divine guidance that nourishes your cup, fills you up, reconnects you.

Then, once you've nourished those two relationships—and these are both nonnegotiables every single day, no matter what, whether it's five minutes or five hours—you're then ready for your third relationship, which is with your tribe. So for you, James, as an example, this is your four angels and your beloved. That's your tribe. Once you've nourished *you*, you're in a better, calmer, more compassionate, loving, kind place to be of service. As a beloved, as a father, and then from there to step into the arena as a professional or [whatever] you do to be of service. (Episode 74)

Those leaders who embraced their crucible grew their self-awareness, integrity, compassion and relatableness, and they excel at learning. Authentic leaders have a drive to learn about who they are, about who their colleagues are, about what their profession is and where their profession is going. They want to learn how they can increase their impact on the organization culturally as well as improve the bottom line. Their stories are told in chapter 6.

Brad Stulberg, who co-authored *Peak Performance: Elevate Your Game, Avoid Burnout, and Thrive with the New Science of Success*, discusses his passion for learning. Brad is less reflective here on the role a particular crucible had in his self-awareness, but if learning is the driver of growth, Brad demonstrates it:

Man, where do I begin. I think probably the number one reason, and it's hard to number them, but one of the predominant reasons that I really like writing is simply because I'm very curious and I love to learn. I think that I have the best job in the world because I get to talk to fascinating people, hear their stories and learn from them, too. There aren't too many other jobs where you get paid to go talk to experts that have dedicated their life [to something], whether it's to a new scientific theory or to the physicality it takes to win gold medals in the Olympics. They want to talk to you, and they want to tell you how they did it. (Episode 32)

Chapter 7 is the wrapping on the present, and where I bring the Authentic Leadership Model into full focus. The leader's drive to learn is what helps guide them on their journey. In this chapter I revisit key themes and present some questions to determine where *you* are on your journey to authentic leadership.

The "So What?"

As I spoke with executives over the last three years, many indicated that the concepts discussed in this book are important for personal development, but that often an argument emerges around how the organization earns money. It can be tough to quantify the outcomes of having a more compassionate workforce or of putting relationships before profits. I get it. Many of the interviewees in this book work for publicly traded companies that are responsible for returning profits to their shareholders. As a result, the whole conversation about organizations acting more authentically inside and out cannot be restricted to leader-follower relationships. The message needs to involve the shareholders, the board and the public in general. However, with a goal of speaking the language of those who hold the financial purse strings, I want to provide some information on the financial "So what?"

According to the Gallup Organization, employees in the U.S. and Canada are engaged only 31 percent of the time, the lowest rate for a workforce in the OECD (Organisation for Economic Co-operation and Development). Globally, the average employee is only 15 percent engaged in the workplace. This varies by region, but overwhelmingly workplace engagement is not a net positive experience. In the U.S., this amounts to a loss of productivity of between $450 and $550 billion.[1] Add to this the $1 trillion a year the global economy loses due to depression and anxiety.[2]

Now, what about those organizations that have high engagement? In the same survey, Gallup found that the organizations in the top quartile of the results have employees who are 17 percent more engaged and that the organizations themselves are 21 percent more profitable than those in the bottom quartile.[3]

Dr. Jessica Grossmeier, the lead researcher, asked a simple question: "Do publicly traded organizations that prioritize employee health and well-being outperform the competition on the stock market?" To answer this question, Grossmeier and her colleagues began with publicly traded organizations that scored high on the HERO Employee Health Management Best Practices Scorecard, which was co-created by the Health Enhancement Research Organization (HERO) and Mercer (a global HR consulting firm). The researchers determined that the cutoff of the seventy-fifth quartile or higher (a score of 125 out of 200) on the HERO scorecard was evidence of a high-performing organization as far as the organization's health and well-being were concerned.

After determining which organizations would be included in the research project, the research team explored how the forty-two chosen organizations compared to organizations on the S&P 500 on a simulated stock market for 2009 to 2014. This is where explaining the nuances of the experiment becomes difficult, and I encourage you to read the article (see the endnotes), but here is the key takeaway: the team assigned every organization with an initial investment of $10,000, starting in 2009 (they also staggered the investments over three years due to companies completing the HERO scorecard at different periods). Each January, they rebalanced the investment portfolio, to account for any biases due to performance, and reinvested all dividends. They then compared the results of the high-performing portfolio with the S&P 500 during the same period. What they found is that those high-performing publicly traded organizations appreciated 235 percent compared with the S&P500 portfolio appreciation of 159 percent, based on the original investment of $10,000.

Finally, a 2014 study by researchers out of the U.K. found that happiness in the workplace resulted in a 12 percent increase in workplace productivity.[4] Professor Andrew Oswald, Dr. Eugenio Proto and Dr. Daniel Sgroi from the University of Warwick's Department of Economics used randomized trials to find causal evidence that happiness leads to more productivity. Their research included four different experiments with more than seven hundred participants. They conclude that when employees are happier, they use the time given to complete projects more efficiently, resulting in simply getting more done.

The literature is unequivocal, and I could bore you with study after study. I won't, though, because it is clear that organizations are suffering because *people* are suffering. People are not as productive, happy or engaged as they could be. Companies are losing money on the one area where investing in innovation pays off—their human capital. More and more research is coming out showing the positive financial impact of creating a happier and healthier workforce. Taking this a step further, countries such as the United Arab Emirates and Bhutan have dedicated governmental offices that focus on creating the conditions for a healthy and happy citizenry. Research suggests that there is a significant financial impact for organizations that take care of their employees. To be more specific, I believe there is a significant emotional, social, mental and moral impact for organizations when they are led by authentic leaders.

What This Book Is and Is Not

This book was born out of my life nudge and is a reflection of the interviews I culled to help develop the Authentic Leadership Model. At the end of each chapter, exercises are suggested to help you grow your authentic self. These opportunities for growth were developed by my colleagues Dr. Seth Gillihan and Dr. Kara O'Leary. Dr. Gillihan is a clinical psychologist who received his PhD from the University of Pennsylvania and has a practice in Philadelphia, Pennsylvania. Dr. O'Leary received her PhD from Columbia University and is a practicing clinical psychologist in St. Louis, Missouri. Dr. Gillihan and Dr. O'Leary have a combined twenty-five years of experience working with a cross-section of the population who experience anxiety, depression, OCD, abuse and much more.

This book is also about providing you with insight into the humanization of successful C-suite leaders and subject leaders. I have always felt that hierarchies are a necessary evil, but it's one that I struggle with. (That is why, I maintain, the military would never have wanted me.) But when you learn about other people's strengths and weaknesses, successes and failures, you start to see that even the leaders among them are not all that different from you and me. Authenticity can be the great equalizer in human interactions.

Finally, I did not set out to write an academic book. There are many, many academic studies on leadership, and volumes of academic leadership books. You can go to any bookstore, if you still go to one, or go on Amazon and search for leadership titles, and the number will impress you. But as I said, this is not an academic work. I don't list study after study. Rather, I present a concept born out of the interviews that I conducted for my *Executives After Hours* podcast, and at times I turn to literature to excite you to think about your relationship to yourself and others in the context of authentic leadership.

So, sit back, grab yourself something to drink—perhaps a Dewar's on the rocks (currently my favorite nighttime beverage) or any other beverage of choice—and partake of the journey many leaders have taken to be authentic.

(1)

THE CRUCIBLE
THE GIFT OF ADVERSITY

There are things, especially where I am now, where I'm thinking what's next? What's next is what I feel right now is right to do.

CAROLINE GASC, executive coach and former CFO, MPH Global Services (Episode 84)

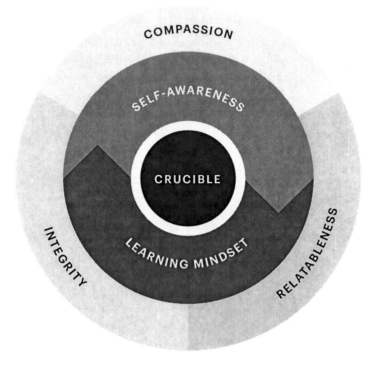

Defining the Crucible

To explore the concept of the crucible, let's turn first to the work of Dr. Warren Bennis, author of the highly acclaimed *On Becoming a Leader*.[1] In the book, Bennis describes a crucible as a discernible experience in which individuals move through one or more events which develop and/or evolve the individual's sense of identity. Or, as I like to say, your world got rocked and you took a moment to take stock of your life, resulting in a fundamental shift in your core identity.

These are life's moments of truth, when a fork in your path is in front of you. Take the one fork and you start down a path of potential self-destruction, self-sabotage and self-loathing. Take the other fork and you start down a path of self-awareness, self-compassion and self-determination.

Let's take the case of Dr. Hal Movius, the CEO of Movius Consulting, Inc. (episode 83). Hal had never contemplated pursuing a PhD or a career in consulting—he was too busy jamming in a rock band. Hal's crucible came when his best friend found out he had cancer. As Hal's friend became more sick and realized he was not going to survive, Hal decided to spend the last three to four months with his friend, who died at 26. It was in the midst of this event that Hal took a long hard look in the mirror and decided, "I am not going to go into the music business. I'm not cut out for that. I'm not single-minded enough. I don't wake up and want to play the guitar nine hours a day and spend another three figuring out how to get tapes into people's hands, and so on."

As Hal was considering a career alternative to rock music, he began to drift towards the idea of law school. But then one night he had a chance meeting with a friend who suggested that he apply for a job as a research associate in an emerging field: negotiation and mediation. He applied for the job on a whim, got it and ended up working with some key mentors in the field of dispute resolution. Eventually he earned a PhD from the University of Arizona and completed a postdoctoral internship at Cambridge Hospital, one of the teaching hospitals of Harvard Medical School. Hal had had one path in front of him, but a life nudge appeared in the form of a crucible and gave Hal a chance to look in the mirror and ask the hard question, "What am I really suited for?"

A "What the??" Moment

I propose that crucibles fall into three buckets. Do you remember the *Seinfeld* episode in which Elaine describes to Jerry that she has a friend who is the exact opposite of him? Jerry says, "So he's Bizarro Jerry!" The first bucket is the *bizarro crucible*. This is all about being put into a new situation that challenges your conventions of "normal." It may be the exact opposite of anything you have ever experienced, and thus can make you very uncomfortable. This is when you should lean in.

Here is a bizarro crucible experience for me. In August 2005, I was 31 and living with my mom—again—and had just been offered admission by the University of Western Australia to pursue my doctorate. I had spent the previous six months calling and emailing Admissions every week to find out if I was accepted. I call this tactic "being pleasantly persistent," as I was always friendly. Leading up to my move, I was consumed with paperwork, visas and packing, and on January 19, 2006, I boarded a plane to Perth, Australia, to begin my new adventure. When I arrived, I was escorted to a dorm room as a temporary place to live until I found an apartment.

When I woke up that first morning, I freaked out. My mental state was less than stable and my thoughts varied from straight-up panic to depression and every emotion in between. They would go as follows: "What are you doing? You are 31 years old, with no job, living in a foreign country." Or "This is pathetic! You don't belong in a PhD program." Or a few choice F-words leading up to "I'm not smart enough!" You get the idea.

To clear my head, I decided to lace up my sneakers and go for a run. I had music blaring in my ears to drown out my thoughts as I headed down Sterling Highway at six in the morning towards Cottesloe Beach. UWA lies next to the Swan River at the bottom of a slight hill, so I was running uphill. I was confused, tired, feeling negative about everything, out of breath and getting ready to turn around and head back to my dorm room to sulk. But when I got to the top of the hill, what I saw changed my life. I am not using hyperbole here for the sake of drama. It literally changed everything.

As I took a deep breath and began to slow down to a walk, I looked up. The sky was a deep blue; the day was crisp, but comfortable; and the smell of ocean engulfed my senses. My eyes locked onto the vast blue of the Indian Ocean and the green of the trees on the coast, and a breeze brushed across my face. I was about two and a half miles from the beach, but I began to run towards it, and with every step that took me nearer to the beach, my anxiety, depression and doubt began to leave my body. The weight of the world felt like it was being taken off my shoulders, put down on the ground and left to rot on its own. In that moment my resilience and flexibility increased. More importantly, that moment allowed me to embrace a new challenge in the face of the unknown.

When a person is inserted into a strange or exotic setting or has an encounter so different that they have no prior experience to measure it against, their senses are sharpened; they become more alert to the information they are taking in, and they process that information quickly to make sense of the situation in the midst of their confusion. Take Daniele Giovannucci, president and CEO of the Committee on Sustainability Assessment. When Daniele was six, his family moved from Italy to Philadelphia. He didn't speak English but was immediately placed in the second grade. Daniele describes the situation like this:

Well, I'll tell you the story of how my first day at school, speaking no English, ended up. In Italy, when I left the first-grade classroom, everybody wore a uniform, like a smock kind of thing, and we had inkwells with an actual . . . pen that you dip, and it was all wood and very "homey," I guess is the word. [I] end up in the U.S. in a cinder-block classroom that was freezing cold in November in 1963.

I never forgot that I was so frustrated 'cause I didn't understand a word that anyone was saying. We'd just arrived two days prior. I didn't have a book or anything, and [the teacher] told the child next to me to hand me a book, at which point I was so frustrated because I also couldn't read it that I had tears in my eyes. He turns around and hands me his textbook, but it is upside down and she insists that I read it.

I could tell that she's asking me that, and I kind of pick [the book] up and I've got tears in my eyes. I can't even see the print and, of course, I'm picking it up, holding it upside down. It's equally useless whether it was right side up or upside down. I'm holding it upside down and the class erupts in laughter, and I was already mortified.

I asked how this made him feel, and his response demonstrates exactly what you would expect of someone going through a bizzaro crucible:

What it led to—and I actually thought about this many years later—was those decision[s] you make as a child that are the best decisions you can make with the opportunity at hand, and . . . you can continue to operate as an adult from that initial decision that goes unquestioned later on in life 'cause it's just buried somewhere back in time. I realized that the decision I took at that point as a boy was "I really don't like this. I've got to be really extraordinary so that nobody ever laughs at me again." (Episode 35)

The second bucket is the *forced break crucible*. Forced break crucibles are those times when life nudges you to take time away from your current reality. These could come in the form of prolonged unemployment, a breakup with a long-term partner, going back to school or embarking on a spiritual journey.

In January 2000, at 26, I was hired to be the branch manager for a national advertising company in San Jose, California. I was tasked with trying to keep the lights on in an office that went from twelve full-time staff down to four. When I took the job, I made one request: that I would no longer make cold calls to find new business. Sales pitches? Cool. Fifty cold calls a day? Maybe necessary, but uncool. Plus there was a full-time sales representative in the office, and I thought, "Great! Now I can lead a group without getting bogged down in making sales calls all day long." After I took the job, however, I found out that the sales representative had been in the office for only a few months over the prior year, and for various HR-related reasons could not be fired.

After a heated debate with my boss, I began making cold calls. Then, on one sunny San Jose afternoon, I clicked on a link in an email. You know, the kind that you *know* you shouldn't click on but your curiosity gets the better of you. Twenty minutes later the entire network went down. I was *that* guy. I believe the final count was twenty-two offices that went black. One month later I was laid off with no severance package, no thank-you-for-trying, nothing. Granted, I had only been at the company for a total of five months, but I had moved to San Jose, and at the time I thought their action was heartless. This was my forced break crucible. I spent the summer teaching adults and kids how to swim, painting walls at a gym, taking daily hikes with my dog and just chilling out.

If you have ever driven in San Jose, you know that rarely do drivers adhere to the speed limit. I was so relaxed that I remember driving up the 880 getting flipped the bird because I actually drove 65 miles an hour in a 65 mph zone. My only response was to wave and smile. Do you remember the *Seinfeld* episode where George has the "summer of George"? This was my summer of George (and the last *Seinfeld* reference of the book—I promise). I took the next three months to recalibrate my goals and my focus, which resulted in a move to Staten Island, New York, to begin my MBA at a small liberal arts college and pursue what I thought was my future—coaching water polo. That didn't pan out, but the forced break crucible pushed me in a new direction and added resilience and flexibility.

When a forced hiatus occurs, whether it is mandated or by choice, you end up in extended periods of contemplation or deliberation in which you are challenged to clarify your values and your purpose in life. There may be no greater forced break in one's life than that illustrated by the Reverend Canon Richard Pengelley, dean of Perth's Anglican Diocese. The Reverend Pengelley was a two-time water polo Australian Olympian who walked away from the sport in his prime to pursue his spiritual calling. In discussing this, he shares the joys of making the Olympic squad and the challenges that led him to choose the priesthood:

[Being an Olympic athlete is] such an enormous commitment, and I wasn't paid. I was an amateur. I was paying for the privilege. I had a family by then. I was working as a sports teacher in schools. Huge, huge commitment, and wonderfully supported by my wife, but I recalibrated, set the goal and in '84 made it. You know, it's very exciting when you've been through that. In '88 I made it again, was the vice-captain, would have become the captain, but then made a decision to walk away because of the demands and because I had a family and because I was called into a specific ministry. (Episode 33)

Typically, we think of crucibles as negative events that can shake us to our core, but as Richard points out, his forced break was due to his desire to serve the church.

The third bucket is the *avalanche crucible*. The avalanche is the crucible when it feels like the whole world is collapsing around you as a result of impairment, defeat, failure, vulnerability and even death, such as the death of someone close to you. Across the 140-plus interviews, I was blown away by how often these crucibles occurred for leaders and how often they chose to use them to make different and better choices.

As you dig yourself out of the avalanche, you learn persistence, perspective and patience with the world around you. The stories of Mo Gawdat (former chief business officer of Google X), Bridgette Mayer (owner of Bridgette Mayer Art Gallery) and Doug Smith (second pick overall in the 1981 NHL hockey draft) represent true avalanche moments.

The Avalanche Crucible for Three Leaders

Mo Gawdat: One Billion Moonshots (Episode 104)

Mo Gawdat has had an amazing career. He started off working for IBM, eventually making his way to Microsoft and then to Google X. By all accounts, looking from the outside, he was on top of the world. He was making a gazillion dollars, traveling around the world solving problems. For example, one of the concepts behind Google X—and this is amazing—is "moonshots": coming up with impossible ideas that have impossible challenges and trying to solve those challenges. One of the impossible ideas Mo was tasked with was finding a way to get internet access to parts of Africa that didn't have any infrastructure or even electricity. His team's solution was to tether hot-air balloons that had wireless connectivity to each other, connecting people to the internet in the middle of nowhere.

This is the sort of stuff Mo did at Google X—some pretty crazy, innovative, fun stuff. Even Mo admits he had the coolest job ever. However, before his crucible, he was very unhappy. His expectation of what he should be (happy) and the reality of what he was (unhappy) created emotional and mental conflict. Mo wanted to be happy, so he set out to *Solve for Happy* (the title of his book). After nearly a decade of doing his own engineering-esque research, Mo believed he had at last solved for happy. This equation would be fully tested with the unexpected death of his son. Mo and his son Ali were the best of friends, often gaming until the wee hours of the morning. However, while at university in the States, Ali was rushed to the emergency room. He needed to have an appendectomy. He passed away at 20 from an unfore-seen complication. As for any parent, for Mo, losing a child was an earth-shattering moment full of "why," "I don't understand" and "fuck! fuck! fuck!"

Mo believes that if he had not taken the time to understand happiness, his son's death would have derailed him. He was sad and depressed, but his belief that happiness depends on your expectations helped him get through a difficult situation. The death of his son proved to be a significant crucible that shifted Mo's beliefs, focus and sense of purpose in life. His goal became getting one billion people solving for happy—one billion personal moonshots. So like a good interviewer should, I asked the obvi-ous question. I asked Mo for his definition of happiness. He said:

I struggled with that in my search for happiness, right? You remem-ber my story is that as a successful young executive and day trader and having a wonderful family, I was miserable. I was happy until I started to engage in life, and when life started to bless me, I started to become more and more unhappy. I couldn't understand the lit-erature available on happiness. It does not speak to the mind of an engineer, does not speak to the mind of an executive.

So I went out to define happiness the only way I knew how, which is in an engineering format. I actually went out and listed all of the moments I could remember where I felt happy, and then I tried to plot a trend line between them, like you would do on a chart, hop-ing that when I found that trend line it would describe an equation [for] happiness. And there are many ways . . . you can say happiness is all about being with people that you love, right? But no. You can be with people that you love but pissed off about the promotion you didn't get. Or happiness is about success in life. No, you can be successful in life but unhappy about being stuck in the traffic jam.

So I kept going through that analogy until I realized that the only common trend I could find was you feel happy when the events of your life seemed to be meeting your expectation of how life should behave. So you can put that in an equation: happiness is equal to or greater than the way you view the events of your life minus your expectations of how life should behave. So every moment you've ever felt happy in your life was a moment where life seemed to be meeting your expectations.

As Mo shared his definition of happiness, I had to look at this through the consumer behavior lens (my academic training was in consumer behavior) to better understand his perspective. The best analogy I could come up with was going to the same restaurant again and again but on many different occasions. These visits create an expectation of the experience at the restaurant: the food, the aromas, the décor, the staff and the wine. All of this creates your service expectation, and when one aspect of that is not fully met, you will become unsatisfied. The point that Mo is making, and that I am trying to articulate, is this: you are happy when in any given situation your expectations are met. However, calibrating your expectations so that you are happy is another concept entirely, and that is why Mo wrote *Solve for Happy*. You're welcome, Mo, for the shameless plug. It's well worth the read.

Bridgette Mayer: Survivor of Childhood Abuse (Episode 91)

Bridgette Mayer is an art gallery owner who has exceeded all expectations that were placed on her as a child. Bridgette is from Philadelphia and owns a gallery in Philadelphia and an art consulting office in Los Angeles, and is the author of *The Art Cure* (her unique story). She is ranked as one of the top gallery owners in the U.S., meaning she has an amazing eye for finding art and artists. Bridgette's story is mind-blowing. Growing up in New Jersey, Bridgette spent her first nine years in and out of foster care before she was adopted. But it was *how* she was living that surprised me. I vividly remember tearing up while she shared with me her story. I'll let Bridgette tell you:

I went through an intense amount of physical abuse as a child. I'm talking about beatings where I was hospitalized and literally left abandoned for a week or two in an apartment with no food and literally drinking water from the toilet bowl because there were no cups and I couldn't reach the sink from infancy until when I left the environment at nine.

When I got out of there and actually went into a normal home, I remember feeling an enormous sense of relief and safety. I think my situation initially probably was different than maybe [that of] the average young person who is being adopted, because there was a lot of violence and abuse and neglect. For me it was okay; I knew intuitively I was in a safe place. I took a shower for the first time, had normal clothes. Had a bed to sleep in—[before,] we were sleeping on the floor in a mattress with six kids.

My birth mother was a drug addict, hardcore alcoholic. She would disappear, she was into prostitution. It was like . . . she just kept popping out babies. We had two fathers—there were six kids originally—and the birth family.

Even after Bridgette got adopted at nine, she realized she was behind the eight ball: "When I got older, it hit me that I was really at a significant disadvantage from the start, and I always felt like I was coming from behind."

Those early years in New Jersey developed Bridgette's character, attitude and grit. Here is what makes Bridgette's story stand out to those who have never been through this type of ordeal. She was adopted with two of her sisters, but unlike her, they continued to struggle with substance abuse, relationships and life in general. What impacted me especially is that when you ask Bridgette why *she* was able to make a fundamental course correction, she attributes a lot to luck and a lot to finding the right people at the right time to give her the life nudge. Now, I don't want to paint the picture that Bridgette had an idyllic life once she was adopted. This was not the case; she struggled to make sense of her past and at times struggled in the present, but somehow, Bridgette's crucible fundamentally shifted her identity and focus to the point where she embarked on a different path.

Doug Smith: From Professional Hockey Player to Quadriplegic Runner (Episode 5)

At the age of 18, Doug Smith was drafted second overall by National Hockey League's Los Angeles Kings. Over the next eleven years, Doug played with many NHL teams. Known to have a chip on his shoulder and at times be difficult to coach, upon reflection Doug believes this was due to his childhood. When he was a child, he was in leg braces—think Forrest Gump—and had to prove that he belonged and, more importantly, could be respected. Though being in leg braces is a crucible, it pales in comparison to what happened to Doug at 29 while playing pro hockey. I'll let Doug talk about his crucible:

DOUG SMITH: I lived in a culture of professional sports. Not just being in professional sports but the journey towards professional sports conditions you. It conditions you to do four things: knock people down, intimidate them, take what they have and then expose every conceivable weakness that you possibly can in front of twenty thousand people.

So that mastery led to me getting very good at sports, getting to the NHL, and then basically seeing the devastation that occurs at that level. I didn't recognize it at the time. I didn't know anything else. And then—when I was 29 years old, after eleven years of playing pro sports, and all these fights, these goals, these assists, the big games—all of a sudden I stumble into the boards at full speed and shatter the fifth and sixth cervical vertebrae in my neck, which resulted in paralysis from the chest down. And I wake up in ICU one day, a quadriplegic: unable to feed myself, unable to clean myself or shower myself, and in a type of pain that people who haven't suffered a spinal cord injury can't possibly relate to.

Well, because I was in a hospital bed for about a year, I was on about 200 milligrams of morphine a day, 25 milligrams of Halcion, which is a knock-out drug. I was in, you know—this was after one, two, three surgeries. So I went from a hospital bed to a spine chair, to a walker, to a cane, to doing exercises, walking exercises, over the course of about, yeah, about twelve to eighteen months.

JAMES: Were you expected to walk again?

DOUG: Well, no. The automatic default for spinal cord injury, or even brain trauma now, because they are all so different, is that you're not going to walk again. If you're there, you're not going to get it back. And here's why. So in the medical system, if they tell you, "No, you're not gonna get better" but you do, well that's just fantastic and that's wonderful. Wow, that's incredible. But if they tell you, "Sure you're gonna get better," and you don't . . . 'cause most of the time you're not going to [recover] as well as you thought you would. But the transition right now in the system is that we're moving to a place where doctors save your life and then there's another place you can go for healing.

So I was in that situation, where my wife was told, my family was told . . . you know sometimes there's doctors out there that feel they need to tell the patient—for some strange reason I haven't been able to understand this—but there are some doctors that need to tell the patient that they'll never succeed. And a lot of times they're proven wrong, but again there's nothing that they can get sued about by telling a patient that.

Today Doug studies, speaks to groups and works with organizations around the concept of trauma. Oh, and he runs—a lot. Doug and many other interviewees give full credit to their crucible as the linchpin of who they are, what they do and how they have grown as individuals. The crucibles listed here are only a small sample of interviews in which a crucible was at the center of transformation, but what are the lessons learned?

Three Lessons

For each crucible—regardless whether it was a bizzaro, forced break or avalanche crucible—there are three lessons that teach how to choose the right response to a crucible, how to increase focus on purpose and how to experience heightened gratitude.

Let's start with choice of response. In my mid-twenties I did a bit of therapy, and one thing I learned is that we cannot control what happens to us but we *can* control how we respond. This was a clear theme for authentic leaders. Without fail these leaders were not derailed by the crucible but rather were empowered by it and able to focus on what was next. It was not "Look at what terrible thing happened to me" but "How can I use this event to move forward and better myself?" That is not to say there was not a period of self-pity, but there came a point where this internal dialogue no longer serves its purpose, and this is when a shift occurs. Ultimately, for these leaders, it came down to perspective and a choice. Bridgette Mayer or Doug Smith could have easily decided that life had dealt them a bad hand and wallowed in their self-pity, leading them on a potential path of self-destruction. The lesson is, it is up to you to choose a positive path, because blaming others for your crucible is a waste of time and energy and only leads down a darker path.

The second lesson revolves around a sense of purpose. Joe Burton, who we met in the foreword and introduction, provides a great example of a leader with a renewed sense of purpose. Joe, at the young age of 40, quit as COO of a large global advertising agency, a decision he took because his personal "well of purpose" felt empty. Like many authentic leaders, he came through his crucible needing more out of life and wanted a purpose greater than an inwardly focused achievement. Daniel Pink, in his book *Drive*, argues that to be intrinsically motivated, a leader needs to have purpose (as well as mastery and autonomy). I found that leaders who came out of their crucible with a positive mindset found a purpose that revolved around something greater than themselves.

Another aspect that emerges is humility. As people like Daniele, Joe, Bridgette and Doug shared their stories, it became less about what they said and more how they said it. As their stories unfolded, they were delivered with an emotional rawness and a respect for life's fragility. As Daniele said, "I've got to be really extraordinary so that nobody ever laughs at me again." It's painful just reading that sentence, let alone living it.

That final lesson drawn from going through a crucible is a growth in gratitude. Regardless of the crucible—and many are jaw-dropping—a leader can come out of the experience stronger, more focused and with a heightened sense of purpose. This results in sincere gratitude for the crucible as opposed to feeling you'd been kicked to the curb.

When I pressed the people I interviewed about takeaways from their crucible, it was this sheer gratitude for the event that made the biggest impact on me. I never sensed resentment or regret. The "woe is me" attitude was absent. They looked at cause and effect in a positive light. Their crucible was always something that, in the moment, they thought was hell, but in retrospect they took positives out of the experience, resulting in a forward-moving positive ripple effect.

My Personal Crucible

My crucibles are no more or less significant than anyone else's, but they are mine, and I wear them like that old ragged T-shirt from your early twenties you still wear. The number of minor and major crucibles that have personally impacted me would require a separate book. At 19, I watched a man die in a car wreck. I remember vividly his last breath, seeing his chest rise and fall as blood came out of his nose, eyes and ears. This event made me appreciate my journey in this world. I have had a relative steal $10,000 on credit cards (not good for my trust) and every minor crucible in between. But there is one crucible at this point in my life that stands out above all others: the loss of my father when I was 20.

I was attending the University of Dayton, in Ohio, and summer break had just begun. I was visiting my then girlfriend, who attended Western Oregon University in Monmouth. We were out for a walk around the campus and had just gone into her dorm when the phone rang. To this day, I can clearly remember how the room was set up. The bunk beds were on the right against the wall; the dressers were on the left at the end of the room; the desks were against the wall in the middle of the room. Now, at this point, my dad had been sick for only about six months with early-onset heart failure, but the prospect of death had not entered the conversation, or at least my parents decided not to share it with me. My guess is that this was done by design to protect me. So while I was talking to my girlfriend, I got a phone call on the dorm phone from a dear family friend, and she simply said, "Your dad passed." There were some other words that followed, but to be fair, I wasn't really listening. Those three words put me on my knees, and buckets of tears came flowing out.

During the next two years, I didn't really deal with the loss. No one around me had dealt with this type of loss either. I often felt alone. So I self-medicated, with excessive drinking. I acted out in ways that showed I was screaming for attention and help, but no one around me really saw it, and to be fair, I didn't know how to ask for help. What I did realize, or want, was to live my life for today. This wasn't always good for the ol' bank account, but I look at my dad's life focusing on the idea that we have only a finite amount of time on this earth and we can't take our money with us when we die, so get out there and live!

Fast-forward twenty years and four kids, and his death has crept back into my psyche. What I have failed to mention is that my dad died at 49. I now find myself driving my career as hard as possible to achieve multiple goals and objectives, because in my mind, I am dead in six short years. Logically, I can see why this is a flawed proposition, but emotionally, for every illness and every visit to the doctors, I look for parallels in my health that signal my "demise." Again, I know this logic is flawed. I'm not overweight like my dad was; I'm active and my dad was not; I eat healthy foods and my dad did not; and, essentially, I am a combination of both my parents' genes. But it just isn't easy, and when I ask others whose parents died early about their experience, they tell me that they are going through or did go through the same process.

It's not all tears for me. My dad's death had a net positive impact on who I am today and the type of husband and father I am. If I'm asked if I would prefer him to be alive, that is clearly a yes. I'm just not sure I would be the person I am today or if I would have accomplished the various achievements that I have. Would this book get written? Would I have lived in Australia for nearly four years? Moved to the Middle East? Be the husband or father that I am now? Probably not, but I don't play "What if?" because if I spent all that time looking back, I would never move forward.

Putting the Crucible Concept into Perspective

I came to the conclusion that some sort of crucible was necessary for a leader to be more authentic. I am sure there will be those who read this who will say I don't know what I'm talking about and that it's not necessary to have a crucible to be authentic. I would expect some readers to say to themselves, "You know, *I* haven't had a crucible." Well, we all have crucibles. It is just their type and significance that vary, sometimes drastically, as does our ability to reflect on them.

Not to be condescending or dismissive, but here is my point: as I noted at the beginning of the chapter, a person's crucible is unique and individual to them, and I am by no means the person to judge what you define as a crucible. All I can do is explain what I found through interviewing a wide-ranging set of leaders. For example, there were CEOs, founders and leaders I interviewed who (at least during the interview) stated that they never really went through any major type of crucible. During these interviews I asked questions that were designed to encourage my guests to reflect on their personal journey. It was just that their answers didn't appear to be very reflective. I could be off with this, and yes, many leaders could just be private individuals—totally possible. However, it seemed to me that my interactions with leaders who denied having a major crucible were at odds with my interactions with leaders who were private but acknowledged a crucible. For example, leaders who were private would either avoid a sensitive topic or state that they didn't want to talk about a particular topic. Meanwhile, leaders who failed to acknowledge a major professional or private crucible didn't avoid my questions and in fact were engaged in any number of topics, but when asked to reflect on their statements, their responses were not thoughtful. Based on these experiences, I came to a simple equation:

Crucible = Authentic Leadership

We will discuss the role learning plays later in the book. But this raises the question: Does a crucible lead to being a successful leader? No, but it helps in gaining perspective.

Final Thoughts (for Now) on the Crucible

As I interviewed one leader after another, and as I thought about my own crucibles, I began to wonder if the type and significance of the crucible had a direct impact on a leader's transformation into a more authentic leader. During my interview with Bill George (episode 114), we discussed the fact that every person has a crucible but that those crucibles differ in their significance. But Bill went on to point out that (and I noted this earlier) every person's crucible is important to *them* and *their* journey.

I started to feel that a *significant* crucible is vital to superior leadership, and that a personal crucible is almost necessary for a leader because it forces reflection. My wife, Mary, and I had a nice debate over this concept—that a crucible and authenticity are inextricably linked—and Mary thinks that one can be authentic without a crucible. My sample is just over 140 deep, but I cannot get past the consistency of *Crucible = Authentic Leadership*. It became abundantly clear to me that leaders who did not have a crucible appeared to have difficulties with their self-understanding.

Earlier I gave a nod to Dr. Bennis for his work in the field of authentic leadership, specifically around crucibles. Bennis and his colleague Dr. Robert Thomas argued in *Harvard Business Review* that a leader gains four essential skills:

1. They are able to relate with others across the organization;
2. They create a distinct perspective that compels their voice;
3. Their identity is connected to integrity and honesty; and
4. They develop the skills of adaptability.[2]

The four skills correlate with what surfaced in my interviews. Further, the skills Bennis and Thomas identify support themes I will discuss in later chapters.

I have proposed a model in which the crucible is at the center of an individual's capability to become more self-aware, compassionate and relatable and to practice higher integrity. It is through the crucible that a leader is provided the opportunity for moments of reflection and growth. However, regardless of the type and significance of the crucible, leaders who want to gain a deeper understanding and improve themselves will seek out help, through personal coaches, books, professional support groups and people significant to them in their personal lives. For me, this was the greatest gift I found through my crucibles, and this was the case for many authentic leaders I interviewed. They told me that they learned to look in the proverbial mirror to gain a better sense of their strengths and weaknesses.

Whether intentionally or not, many authentic leaders I interviewed wore their crucible as a badge of honor—not in an "I'm better than you, nyah nyah" kind of way, but rather as a source of inspiration and hope for others who struggle with their own crucibles. I never felt that they realized they were giving off that vibe, but as their stories unfolded, I could hear them weigh up the significance. For me this is one of the things that continues to fuel my drive to do the *Executives After Hours* podcast.

Where Are We Going Next?

It is in a crucible that opportunity is created for a leader to pause and reflect. It is in that moment of reflection that a leader has their greatest opportunity to develop and deepen their self-awareness. Self-awareness—difficult at times, confronting at times, and necessary all the time—is discussed in the next chapter. The discussion around self-awareness provides context and direction for a leader's ability to create moments of change and growth.

(2)

SELF-AWARENESS

PUBLIC VERSUS
PRIVATE SELF

The big lesson that my kids have taught me is what is important in life. I've come to the conclusion it's not the awards you get or the things you own; they have taught me, it's relationships, not only with them, but with all the people I come in contact [with]. The most important thing is the relationship and [that] I am reaching out and touching people in a positive way.

RON WIENS, leadership coach and organizational change agent (Episode 45)

Do You See What I See?

We all know leaders who, when the wheels come off the bus, refuse to take responsibility but instead start throwing tire irons at the people around them. The blame game hurts a leader's credibility and trust with their colleagues, and can result in harm to the organization's culture. The authentic leader has the desire and ability to look inward during and after a crisis moment. This chapter explores the process of self-reflection and assessment, provides examples from an authentic leader's perspective and offers strategies for becoming more self-aware. Before we get to the meat of the chapter, however, while we all have a concept of what self-awareness is, let's take some time to define it.

What Is Self-Awareness?

A commonly held definition of *self-awareness* is "a transformative process of self-reflection and introspection" by which "through reflection an individual [is] led to clarity in self-assessment. At the end of that, the idea of self-awareness suggests that it's a process whereby one comes to reflect one's unique values, identity, emotions, goals, knowledge, and talents"; often self-awareness "is triggered by external events."[1] Essentially, self-awareness is knowing who you are, what you excel at and where you need to improve to gain a better understanding of your self-concept (a term I'll define in a moment). Authentic leaders can admit to their weaknesses, ask for help and strengthen the team around them by helping the team better understand its strengths and weaknesses. A high degree of self-awareness separates average leaders from authentic leaders.

Self-awareness is also an integral aspect of the proposed model: a leader really needs self-awareness to reflect on the roles that compassion, integrity and relatableness play in their core belief structure. Consequently, as we discuss self-awareness, it is important to keep in the back of your mind that one function of the crucible is to drive the leader to be more self-aware of their strengths *and* weaknesses. The practice of compassion, integrity and relatableness thus becomes deliberate in the daily life of the authentic leader.

Before we dive into authentic leaders and the link to self-awareness, I want to first distinguish the difference between one's self-concept and the process of being self-aware. Self-concept is how you see yourself. For example, I see myself as an outgoing individual who is a husband, a dad, a small-L liberal, athletic and, most relevant, bald. This does not mean that this is how others see me (I will get to that shortly). Self-awareness, on the other hand, is process of reflection of who you are as a person. Mary claims that I may be the most introspective, self-aware individual she has ever met. I spend a large amount of time contemplating who I am and what role I play in society—probably an unhealthy amount, to be honest.

Here's another example: If you ask a female CEO to define herself, she may say she is an athlete, mom, sibling, company executive and leader. She is conscious of her self-concept. If you asked her to share with you how she evolved as a person and a professional from age 25, she would most likely offer a rich and deep description of how she grew and transformed over the years. Essentially, self-awareness requires a sense of honest reflection that arises from a moment in time, and self-concept is about being—"I am this, therefore I am."

Do You Have a 15 Percent Rule?

To be self-aware, you need to be honest with yourself and honest with others. When it comes to "the self," this is an evolutionary process, as life is a journey and not a destination. Because of this, while conducting the interviews for the podcast and this book, I often found myself wondering if the executives I was interviewing were giving me an altered version of their true self. Call this my natural skepticism, as I have found that sometimes individuals in a position of authority and power will engage in "impression management" for their public persona. This leads to leaders who act one way in public and another in private.

This idea of public versus private self is derived from the work of John Turner and his colleagues. Dr. Turner, a well-known social psychologist who led the development of self-categorization theory, describes self-concept as consisting of two parts. One part is personal identity (how you see yourself); the other is social identity (your belief about how others see you).

About 95 percent of us engage in the public-private battle to either control or fulfill how others see us as an individual. The other 5 percent of us, I believe, are either super authentic—off-the-charts real at all times—or sociopathic, but I am not here to judge. This leads me to my 15 percent rule. Being 100 percent authentic all the time is an ideal, and as such is not realistic. We are human, and life is complicated and rich with our personal history and stories we might never choose to make public. Staying within 15 percent of your authentic self should be the goal. What I mean by this is that if a person is truly authentic, they will have a baseline of authenticity (which requires self-awareness), but they will also have the ability to turn their authentic self up or turn it down.

For example, I have a tendency to be overly honest with people, even when a person is not asking for my opinion—it's the ol' unsolicited advice sharing syndrome, better known as OUASS. This requires me to read the situation (to be self-aware) and change my tactic to be more question focused. Authentic leaders understand when to be true to their authenticity, especially under the umbrella of compliance that requires them to be highly self-aware and to regularly take time to reflect and evaluate their baseline of personal authenticity.

However, there have been times when I have met a guest after they appeared on my show only to find the interaction to be completely different when the microphone isn't turned on. They didn't have a 15 percent rule. During the interview, they would turn up the public self and engage in impression management. They were funnier, more engaging and more "present," if you will, but off mic they came across as if (1) their agenda had been met and (2) their agenda had been served.

Now I need to note (and my wife Mary would verify this) that I am hypersensitive to these types of encounters and may be reading into them. Others could be engaging in their 15 percent less authentic self, and this represents a full 30 percentage point swing. I have learned to trust my gut in these situations, and to me these individuals are not authentic leaders but charismatic leaders.

Let's take a different perspective on the public self/private self dilemma. Imagine you have a dominating public self, so you engage in psychological impression management to the highest levels. This includes the way you relate to leadership, to your team, and to other external individuals or teams. Then, when the day is over, you go home and take a 180-degree turn and act the opposite way. You sense that there's no pressure to be or act in a particular way. You almost feel like the weight of the world gets put on the shelf until the next working day, and then the act begins all over again.

For those who engage in some version of this, it is exhausting—mentally, physically, emotionally, even spiritually, *and* your team sees it for what it is. In many cases, your team will be a witness to the theater. It is because of this act that trust is eroded. When public and private personas are far apart, you're actually less authentic. It's confusing for you as an individual to understand the reasoning behind why you act one way at one time and another way another time. The goal should be to narrow the gap between the public and private selves. The closer together they are, the greater the chances that you are more authentic professionally and personally. Remember, 86,400 hours of your life are spent at work.

What Did They Say about You at Your Funeral?

David Brooks, a *New York Times* op-ed columnist, is the author of the book *Road to Character*, in which one of the many topics he covers is the concept of résumé versus eulogy virtues. *Résumé virtues* are the skills that the marketplace desires, while *eulogy*

virtues are the things that will be talked about at your funeral—
virtues like kindness, love, empathy, integrity, joy, loyalty and
many more. I explored an interesting way to test the public versus private self by asking my interviewees how they wanted to be
thought of after they are no longer among the living. I would ask,
"What do you want people to say about you at your funeral?" or
a second version of the question, "What do you want inscribed
on your headstone?"

Dennis Boyle, co-founder and partner at IDEO, said he would
like to be remembered with words like these: "Well, he was just
good at a lot of things... Good spouse, a good father, a good
son, a good brother, a good designer, good teacher. And kind
and compassionate and funny and smart... Left a legacy with a
bunch of people that loved and admired him and accomplished
some unique things... in his work from an innovation standpoint" (episode 99).

James Poer, CEO of Kestra Financial, stated, "I would want
my kids to say that they were loved and that I helped make them
a better person. I would hope my wife would say that I was a
great husband and did well by her and that she felt loved. I would
hope that the people that I have spent loads of time with in my
career would have felt that I made a difference in the industry
that I'm in and helped people in their lives to get to the next level
to be a better person, to challenge themselves, whatever it may
be" (episode 97).

Lisa Buckingham, chief human resources officer for Lincoln
Financial, reflected on this question and said, "I made a difference. I made a difference. I want to make others feel how much
potential they have. From a tombstone perspective at work,
right. Then I was a good mom. Good mom is a really important
thing to me. I love my son" (episode 71).

This is only a small sample, but the point is that in the roughly
fifty times I asked this question, it was always interesting to

see if the leader's behavior and attitudes during the interview matched their desired legacy. It is in these moments that the leaders showed their true colors when it came to self-reflective ability and exploring their public versus private self.

Don't Let Fear Conquer Your Self-Awareness—Conquer Your Fear

There's a motto that I share with my children and that I try to live by: "Don't let fear conquer you—conquer your fear." The emotion of fear has a wide-ranging impact on our psychological well-being and is at the center of so many of our choices, from moving to a new city or accepting a new job to choosing where to go on vacation and even what we watch on our favorite device. Fear blocks our ability to be fully self-aware, and consequently it becomes tough to be authentic in work and in life outside work. Brené Brown's book *The Gifts of Imperfection* is not only a great read but also uncovers why self-awareness and authenticity are so hard to achieve. Brown states, "It makes sense to me that the gifts of imperfection are courage, compassion, and connection."[2] It would seem to me, then, that the ability to embrace self-awareness is to acknowledge fear of the truth, the shame of your past and your weaknesses.

We have all been in a situation where being our self is scary, and fear of being judged by our peers is paralyzing. Take a moment, close your eyes and recall an instance when you entered a room or a meeting as the "new person." What was your biggest fear? Not being liked? Being judged by how you look? Not fitting in? These fears (and more) are valid, but what is important is what you do with them. For me, the fear is how I look. Super shallow, I know, but my parents were overweight (especially my dad) and to this day I am self-conscious about my weight and how I'm perceived. If I were totally authentic, I wouldn't worry about my appearance and control only what I can, such as what I eat and how much exercise I get.

So what does fear have to do with self-awareness and authentic leadership? As I noted in chapter 1, I believe that being authentic does not begin and end on the job, and many of us have a desire to be authentic across all time and space. However, being an authentic leader in an organizational context has a separate set of fears. Most notably, there is a belief out there that a leader needs to have all the answers. This is so far from realistic that I might as well suggest that I have a full set of hair on my head (please see my author photo). Having all the answers is simply not possible. However, the fear of others perceiving us as less than competent can be a hit on our ego.

Authentic leaders embrace the unknown as they put their pride aside for the greater good of the situation. But this occurs only when we acknowledge our fears, conquer our fears and look inward to gain a greater understanding of what is holding us back. What does it look like for those I interviewed? Let's see.

Three Perspectives on Self-Awareness from the Top

Greg Justice, CEO of National Corporate Fitness Institute (Episode 17)

In addition to his CEO role at National Corporate Fitness Institute, Greg Justice has written a number of books. He has spent the better part of twenty-five years in the health and fitness industry, blazing his own trail. But like many of the leaders I interviewed, Greg had a moment where a crucible created a fork in the road and forced him to look inward. He decided that his health was more important than the short-term gains of working in a mine.

GREG JUSTICE: My sophomore or junior year, my father, at age 49, died of a massive heart attack. I kind of started to look at my life and think, okay, I'm going to die of a massive heart attack or I'm going to get black lung and die at an early age. You know, I'm just thinking, this just doesn't make sense to me. I mean, I was doing it because you could make a lot of money in the coal mines. Believe it or not, coal miners make a lot of money, and I was making enough to buy a hot rod sports car, a Datsun 280Z, in the early eighties . . .

Well, you know, your purpose is oftentimes found right on the other side of passion, right? When my father died, I just kind of started to go into a lot of introspective thought and just thinking, man, I can't do this for the rest of my life. I can't go five miles into the earth and shovel coal out. It just was killing me. I got back to my ultimate passion, which was athletics and sports and exercise science. I will also say that through that time of coal mining technology, I had a stellar 1.4 GPA. No passion, no purpose—I was just doing it for the money. Then a quick turnaround came after my father died; I changed my major.

JAMES: How old were you when your father died?

GREG: Twenty-one years old. I had just turned 21. Yeah, well, you know, that just really, as a young man, I mean, you think you've got your parents there to keep you accountable and to always be there for you, and it just was totally different without my dad there. I knew I had to make a change.

Using his crucible as a stepping stone to live a healthy lifestyle was no easy task, but when faced with mortality, Greg said, it helped him make his decision. In the interview, we also talked about his brother, who is overweight and has a similar physical disposition to his father but who, instead of living a healthier life, decided taking drugs to reduce cholesterol was a better choice. I can only infer, but it would seem to me that when their father died, Greg's brother was not impacted the same way Greg was.

Mark Crowley, Leadership Expert and Former Senior Vice President of Sales Leadership at Washington Mutual (Episode 45)

I loved interviewing Mark Crowley, author of *Lead From the Heart: Transformational Leadership for the 21st Century*, and former senior vice president of sales leadership at Washington Mutual. I have had many great guests, but Mark was one of the best because of his transparency. Mark's mom passed away when he was a child, and as if that was not a significant enough event in his life, his dad was a top-ranking General Electric executive, and Mark described him as almost evil. He spoke about the level of abuse, mostly emotional and psychological, when he was growing up. When Mark went off to university, he often felt alone and longed to be a part of a family that was like a mini-community. Like others I interviewed, Mark went one direction, while a sibling went another; in this case, it was his twin brother:

JAMES: You obviously come from this traumatic and stressful upbringing. How do you think that you went in one direction but your twin brother went in another?

MARK CROWLEY: That's an amazing question. I don't know the answer. I'll tell you what I think. What happened was—I'm going to circle back to this. What happened was that when I was particularly in my last couple years of school, I started to see kids that I was going to school with, not [with] financial advantages, although they certainly had that. They just had people who had their back. They had parents sitting down, talking to them, what classes they were taking.

I remember going in to see the professor. I was a literature major. I sat down with my professor and he goes, "Where do you think you are?" I said, "Well, I think I'm starting my junior year." He goes, "No, man, you're not. You're going to need another year." I'm like, "I need five years to go to school here?" He goes, "Yeah, because you've been taking classes that just don't add up." I just wasn't being guided, you know?

It was just those kinds of things. I used to think ... "What if I'd been more thoughtfully directed? What if I'd had a place to go to on the holidays? What if I'd have had somebody encouraging me and just believing in me and all those kinds of things?" I had plenty of time to have that fantasy, but what happened was, when I started to manage people ... I graduated. I got into my first job. I started managing people. Unconsciously, I started to say, "What if I just gave people what I always wanted and see what the effect would be? I know it would have had a profound impact on my success, so I'm kind of thinking it would have an effect *on everyone's success.*" That's exactly what happened, except I wasn't rational. It was completely unconscious, for a long, long time.

I was in my forties when a woman who had been working for me for about fifteen years said to me, "You realize you manage people very differently, right? You know you approach this unlike anyone else?" I started to say, "What does that mean and what does that look like?" So I started asking people to flesh that out for me. I started to get a real understanding, and again, I think I was 43 years old when I started having these conversations. I started to realize that everything that I had been doing was in response to how I grew up.

I said, "Okay, now that I understand what this is, I want to master this. I want to really refine this, because if this really has this amazing effect on people ..." which it did—incredible engagement, incredible loyalty. People beating a path to work for me. Doing unbelievable work. Scaling mountains for me, consistently. It didn't matter what business I was running or what job they were doing, I had enough evidence that this was really working.

As I ended up writing in the book, I think this is my purpose. I think this was what I'm supposed to be doing. I guess my brother has a different purpose. I don't know what that is, to be honest with you, but that's really what I've convinced myself.

Chris Boyce, Founder and Vice Chairman at Virgin Pulse (Episode 27)

Virgin Pulse is a global corporate wellness provider that works with global organizations on creating mechanisms to help employees be healthier and happier. Chris Boyce, its founder and vice chairman, is a leader who comes from a very strong family, and I am sure he had several personal crucibles, but he spoke of none that was as challenging or even tragic as those of others I interviewed. Chris's crucibles came in his professional career, where he typically works with start-ups or organizations early in their life cycle. It was in these organizations that Chris's self-awareness was honed, because it was obvious to him that to take a company to the next level, he would need to assess his own strengths and weakness:

JAMES: I think that's a really interesting point when you talk about knowing what you know and knowing what you don't know and having the courage and confidence to bring in people to support that. Was that a difficult place to get to, or are you humble enough to know, yeah, I'm not good at new product development?

CHRIS BOYCE: First of all, I'm not humble. It's one of those . . . I wish I were more, but I'm probably not humble. I'm pretty good at intuition and intuitively understanding. I guess for me what I've been able to do was see the broad alignment first before I get into the depth of things, and make sure the broad alignment is right. What I mean by that is broadly aligned: what I cared most about at Upromise was getting the model right and making sure it was successful. My mindset was whatever it takes to do that, that's what I'm gonna do, [even] if that meant bringing in people that were better than me in a lot of things. And there's a lot of people better at a lot of things than me. That was useful.

Knowing what you're not good at and surrounding yourself with great people is one of those things that I think is a key to success.

I've been fortunate enough to be able to do it there at Upromise, fortunate enough to do it here at Virgin Pulse right now as well.

Chris Boyce's professional success in part comes from his ability to understand that the best authentic leaders need to take stock of their skill set and bring in people who can offset their weaknesses, all with the aim of bettering the organization's mission and vision. For Chris, it is through professional crucibles that he continues to grow his self-awareness and succeed. I would also add, regardless of Chris stating that he is not humble, you have to be pretty humble to admit your weaknesses.

What Do These Stories Have to Do with Self-Awareness?

When you read these three narratives or listen to any of the *Executives After Hours* podcasts, you'll find that one thing connects individuals who are high in self-awareness versus low: the crucible. As noted in chapter 1, we all have had crucibles, and we will have more, but our level of awareness is based in the type and severity of our crucibles. For most leaders, the more emotionally raw the crucible, the higher the likelihood they will become more self-aware.

Let's take Greg Justice. Greg faced a clear fork in the road, chose the harder path and made health and fitness his life's work. Mark Crowley had a father who was successful in business but who was devoid of any compassion or love for his kids. Mark took this upbringing, flipped it on its head and made a different choice. But it was the advice of one of his employees about his leadership style that truly pushed Mark to follow his passion: leading from the heart. Finally, Chris Boyce came to realize early on that he couldn't possibly know everything in and about an organization and that he needed to surround himself with people who were better than him in areas in which he was weak. Chris doesn't speak of any major personal crucible, but he gives thanks for his countless professional crucibles.

Greg, Mark and Chris had the wherewithal to pause, be honest with who they were at those various moments and grow. They took stock of their self-concept and goals and had the sense to have people around them who wanted to help.

How Does Self-Awareness Impact Me?

Self-awareness is at the essence of who I am. It has played a significant role in my personal development and impacted my success as a leader. I was the youngest of three and a half children (long story) by five years, and my brothers were competitive swimmers. Anyone who has grown up in a swimming family knows that a swimming family eats, sleeps and lives swimming. Couple that with parents who both worked full-time and were exhausted on the weekends, and by third grade I was a latchkey kid. This combination resulted in a lot of alone time in my own head—great for the imagination, not so great for the negative self-talk as an adult.

This ability to be self-aware came into play in 2000. I mentioned in the last chapter that I have had ten to fifteen crucibles, some deeper and more impactful than others. In 1998 I had a big one. This occurred in my first job after a year of graduate school, when, somehow, I was hired to open the forty-first office of Nationwide Advertising Services (NAS).

Now, to be clear, I was not qualified, but I took the concept of "fake it until you make it" to a new level. One of the perks of the job was a company car. It was a forest green 1998 Honda Accord, by far the nicest car I had driven (clearly excluding the sweet

Toyota Sienna minivan). To put the icing on the cake, I was 25 years old and living with my mom—amazing for the dating life. One fair summer evening I went out for the night, and since my prefrontal cortex was still in development, my decision making was not the best. My mom lived near the Oregon state border in Washington, and I drove to Portland for the evening. After a few too many drinks I drove home. My mom's house was about three miles off the highway, and there's a stretch in the road with an S-turn. At about one in the morning, I vividly remember thinking I was Formula One driver Mario Andretti going through the turn at a high rate of speed. As I recall I was going 70 mph in a 35 mph zone—not safe on many levels.

Just as I navigated through the S-turn, I saw a police car with its lights flashing going in the opposite direction. As I looked in the rear-view mirror, the police car made a quick U-turn. In my mind, I was in a race to get home, get out of my car and get into the house before the police car caught up with me. I made it to my mom's house, and so did the police. My mom's is a typical suburban neighborhood—identical houses, just painted different colors, but all well done with manicured yards and two-car garages. So here I am in a quiet neighborhood drawing unwanted attention.

Now, I am my mom's pride and joy for too many reasons to disclose here, but as I was being taken out of the company car and handcuffed, it was my mom's new boyfriend who came out of the house. This was one of the first times he had stayed the night, and I had only met him one other time. I was fairly embarrassed by this point. But let me add another layer of embarrassment, probably more for my mom's sake than mine: the new boyfriend was standing there in his tighty-whities and a Hanes T-shirt, trying to figure out what was going on. I was now hyper-mortified.

Fast-forward to the self-awareness part. A few weeks later I was in court, and the judge looked at me, I think he saw that I was a productive human being in society, and I had no previous record. He said that if I fulfilled a set of court-mandated requirements, the incident would be expunged from my record. The outcome was a two-year outpatient program broken down into three parts. In the first six months, I attended an outpatient substance abuse group therapy session for three hours a night, three evenings a week. In the second six months I attended once a week for three hours. Finally, I had to see a psychologist for twelve months.

Many people may have tried to find a way out of this, especially in the final twelve months. However, I felt that there was a clear choice: be the victim or be an opportunist. I chose to be an opportunist. I thought that if I have to do this, I need to embrace the process. I wanted to learn more about myself as a human being: what makes me tick, my strengths and weaknesses. I wanted to change my core values, beliefs and attitudes towards life in general.

For the first six months, I spent nine hours a week at an outpatient facility with a group of men and women who were addicts. I spent time telling stories about myself, getting feedback from the group and the counselor. At the end, it allowed me to learn that (a) honesty is an important part of who I am; (b) my emotional intelligence was directly tied to a lack of self-confidence; (c) I am smarter than I thought; and (d) about a hundred other things. Did getting a DUI and going to therapy provide the kind of new level of enlightenment one gets by spending a year with a shaman? No, but it was a great start. It also helped me process my father's death and the impact it had on many of my choices.

The Self-Awareness Void

I started out this chapter describing the leader who places blame and never takes accountability. It is these leaders who provide the biggest lessons in terms of authenticity and self-awareness.

In part, being unauthentic, by definition, means having low self-awareness. In my interview with Ron Wiens, I asked him about a time he fired a client. Ron's response provides one example of his ex-client who lacks self-awareness. I'll let Ron describe it:

The ego was so large. The client would say, "I want you to come in and I want you to build a culture where my people feel committed and involved, and have ideas and put them onto the table." As soon as somebody did that, she would rip them apart and slam them down and threaten to fire them. At that point in time, I said, "This is a bridge too far." Life is too short. That's a big lesson to learn: you have to know when to pull the plug because you can spend a lot of time spinning your wheels. They'll pay you but what you've delivered and the [little] difference you've made is not worth the sweat.

I went on to ask why he thought she was so mean. Ron replied:

Ego is a direct result . . . The larger your ego, the lower your self-esteem. The need to be the first . . . This is what I see almost universally, is that what we call normal performance is actually grossly suboptimal performance. You haven't asked me the prime question: "What is a high-performance culture?" A high-performance culture is one that has three times the productivity of a "normal" culture, and the vast majority of organizations fall under the bell curve of normal culture. (Episode 54)

Lack of self-awareness can manifest itself as passive-aggressive behavior. As Brené Brown suggests, fear is a powerful weapon that can cause individuals to act in ways that others may not. Some leaders who are passive-aggressive are so as a way to be nonconfrontational. They fear that being honest will make either them or the person they're dealing with uncomfortable, but usually it's about them.

Leaders who have low self-awareness make tons of excuses as to why they fail. In essence, they lack accountability. How many of us know a colleague who lacks accountability and is quick to pass the blame? "Hey, Johnny, I didn't receive the spreadsheet last night." "Timmy didn't get me all the data on time." The lack of accountability and acceptance of one's own mistakes is a symptom of a larger issue.

In leaders, being controlling can also be a sign of low self-awareness. These leaders don't have trust in themselves or in the people around them. For example, someone who is controlling may dictate verbatim how they want a project done even if it's a less efficient way, or they may think that their way is the only way something can get done, meaning that they don't trust other people's opinions, perspectives and thoughts about how to complete a project in a different way. They are among the micro-managers.

However, I don't want to make a blanket statement that everyone who is controlling is a micro-manager or is not self-aware. I've talked to a lot of leaders on my podcast who would agree that they're micro-managers and very controlling. So they, at least, are aware of that characteristic. Yet it doesn't define them in terms of self-awareness. In fact, I would argue it actually makes them *highly* self-aware, and it's what they do with it afterward that is more important. It's the leader who *doesn't* know that they are a bully or defensive or passive-aggressive, unaccountable or controlling who is concerning from a self-awareness standpoint.

A handful of leaders I interviewed, when asked what advice they would give their 25-year-old self, didn't have any advice to give. This left me asking, "How can someone be alive for thirty or forty years, past the age of 25, and not have any advice? How is that even possible?" When I went back through the transcripts, I found that during our interviews they didn't speak of having had any significant crucible. The only conclusion I could come up with is that individuals who couldn't give themselves advice to their 25-year-old self have failed to actually self-reflect on one of their crucibles.

Finally, leaders who tend to have the over-ability bias can fall into the category of people with low self-awareness. Have you ever come across the person who swears they are best at X? They exude an overabundance of confidence that doesn't match their ability. I always think of the guy who says he is awesome at basketball, so you say, come play in my pickup game, only to find out your 10-year-old is better. The incongruence between stated ability and reality can get leaders in trouble.

Final Thoughts (for Now) on Self-Awareness

Warren Bennis, Bill George and Karissa Thacker, all authentic leadership experts, suggest that developing self-awareness is the most important and difficult task for an authentic leader. In conducting interviews, I find myself drawn to the leaders who are transparent and self-reflective. To me, it makes the conversation real, not a manufactured impression management experience. What connects these interviews is the role that the crucible played in their life, and their ownership of it. The interviewees would all agree that the crucible plays an important role in developing self-awareness. However, developing self-awareness is easier said than done.

One final note on self-awareness. As I noted in chapter 1, the relevancy to and importance of a crucible in developing a leader's self-awareness are debated. I would agree that this is not an either-or situation, and there are leaders who possess high self-awareness but have never had a major crucible. Yet I would guess that, as I said, and as Bill George believes, everyone has had some type of crucible. The question is, do they know it when it happens and did they reflect on it at some point?

Let's Work on Increasing Self-Awareness

Like any good business or self-help writer, it is my goal to leave you with some actionables. For several chapters of this book, I asked my good friends and colleagues Dr. Seth Gillihan and Dr. Kara O'Leary to help. For this chapter, Dr. Gillihan, Dr. O'Leary and I have six suggestions to offer. Some are mainstream and some are not, but in either case we wanted to create a menu of tools for you to choose from so that you can discover which tools work best for you.

1. *Be mindful for your mind.* Mindfulness is king, and it has been around for centuries. For me it is something that I am personally developing. Even as I write this book, I try to take several one- to two-minute mindfulness breaks during the day when I lose focus. For beginners, I would recommend using an online platform. Personally, I use Whil.com. I interviewed the CEO, so I have an affinity for the product. Headspace.com is an alternative. If neither of these is your cup of tea, try to take a few minutes a day and reflect inward, taking the time to reflect on your day.

    Body scanning (e.g., soundcloud.com/hachetteaudiouk/meditation-two-the-body-scan) is a physically focused method of mindfulness. Use body scanning to increase bodily awareness, which you can practice in any situation. For example, notice what happens in your body when someone irritates you. Learn to recognize what's happening within you mentally and emotionally by being more connected with your body.

    The science is pretty clear when it comes to mindfulness, and the benefits are impactful. In addition to reducing stress and presentism, mindfulness increases awareness and blood flow to the brain. I was surprised by how many of the leaders I interviewed were practicing some sort of mindfulness before mindfulness was a thing to practice. For a deeper understanding of the impact, I recommend reading Joe Burton's book, *Creating Mindful Leaders*.[3]

2. *Beg for feedback.* When I asked authentic leaders how, besides mindfulness, they practice self-awareness, feedback was second. Accepting feedback is hard, even painful. But this necessary evil makes you a better leader and a better person. From an organizational perspective, 360-degree feedback is the most beneficial. This helps you have a better understanding of how your colleagues perceive you. Remember, the closer your public self is to your private self, the more authentic you become.

   If you are trying to develop personally, join a support or accountability group. This can come in the form of a mastermind group, a religious group, or a group of peers you respect and who you know will provide you with honest feedback.

3. *Keep a journal of your thoughts.* When you have felt a shift in your emotions—sadness, jealousy, envy, anger, fear—what went through your mind just prior to the shift? Chances are there was a thought that led from an event to an emotion. Try to use a journal to track your thought-emotions connection when your emotions shift. What was the situation when the shift occurred? What was it about the situation that was uncomfortable? What was the immediate thought that preceded the emotion?

4. *Do the eulogy exercise.* I asked many leaders what they want people to say about them at their funeral. You can do the same thing by writing down what you would like someone

to deliver at *your* funeral. What would you want people to say about you when all is said and done? Now think about your life. To what extent are you living the values you want to have embodied? If you find a discrepancy, what can you do today to change and become closer to the version you want?

5. *Where does your time go?* Create an awareness of how you spend your precious time. Log your activities every day for three days. For each activity, note on a scale of 1 (low) to 10 (high) how much you enjoyed the activity and how important the activity was. For example, TV might be an 8 for enjoyment and a 3 for importance, while doing the dishes might be a 3 and an 8. After three days, take stock of how much of your time you're spending doing things that bring some sense of reward into your life.

6. *Watch yourself.* If you're like me, you find writing a journal difficult. Try to take time to see your patterns and learn your habits, your impulses and the ways you respond to others and others respond to you. This is self-knowledge, and understanding your patterns can help you create plans for you and your team that set you up for success. For example, if you are a big-picture, visionary-type leader and are less skilled at details, it's important that you have others on your team who are very detail oriented.

Where Are We Going Next?

I find myself thinking, if, as a society, we were all more self-aware, would we become neurotic? Maybe, but I guess we would be aware of that, too. In either case, I have found that, without a doubt, authentic leaders I have interviewed are dedicated to increasing their self-awareness by using assessment as a tool and implementing the results. For a majority, the forced reflection has been thrust upon them by a crucible, but at the end they had the ability to learn and grow. This led me to think of my written representation of the model and make a small change:

$$\text{Crucible} = \Delta SA = \text{Authentic Leadership}$$

So, if the impact of crucible equals a change (Δ) in self-awareness (SA), then what is the outcome for a leader who is self-aware? The answer to this question is explored over the next three chapters. While I interviewed leaders for this book a set of macro concepts bubbled to the surface time and again. I found that, in no particular order, integrity, compassion and relatableness impacted an individual's desire to be more authentic with those around them. Let's begin with integrity.

(3)

INTEGRITY

DO + SAY = TRUST

LARRY CHAPMAN: *I was a paperboy. I used to get up at four o'clock in the morning and deliver the papers. I would fold them all and put them in the carrier that I had on my bike, and then I would go on my route.*

JAMES: *What did that job teach you?*

LARRY: *That job taught me that if I wanted to accomplish something, I have to focus, whether the things that I needed to accomplish were getting more subscriptions, to ruffle the feathers of a customer that I had. I had to focus to make sure that I accomplished what it was [that was required]. I think that's probably one of the biggest things. That and probably the issue of consistency, just being consistent. Showing up, doing it, getting up at four o'clock in the morning, getting my route done. It was raining, I had to protect my papers. I had to put wax paper around them. That's probably the two things.*

LARRY CHAPMAN, CEO, Chapman Institute (Episode 63)

71

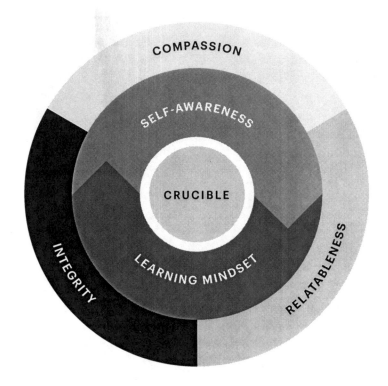

What Is Your Integrity Statement?

Larry Chapman shared with me how he developed his behavioral integrity during his first job as a paperboy around the age of 12. Larry's is a familiar story that kept poking its head up as I asked over seventy leaders about their first job. Over 60 percent of the leaders I interviewed indicated they began working when they were between 10 and 14—and continued to do so. Even at such a young age, many leaders, I discovered, sowed the seeds for behavioral integrity. Behavioral integrity is an important half of the story in creating an integrity statement.

Bill George puts some meat on the bones of integrity when he describes how integrity supports the authenticity of leaders. As noted in chapter 1, George is the author of two books on authentic leadership (*True North* and *Authentic Leadership*). He tends to refer to integrity in three ways. First, he describes it as a genuine expression of one's identity and not the act of mimicking other leaders. Second, he says, integrity is based in honesty: tell the truth and only the truth. Finally, integrity is about fulfilling your role to meet the needs of the larger group, regardless of the temptation to cut corners, and still have some measure of success. Integrity involves honesty, a commitment to follow through and wholeness. We'll explore these concepts next.

Honesty, Relationships and Integrity

The Truth Teller

I have a simple philosophy I try to live by: "Do unto others as you want done to you." I'm not perfect, but one of my core values is honesty, and I try to always be honest. Across 140-plus interviews, the expression and relevance of honesty was a trait my guests spoke to that jumped out at me. Three examples who stand out are Joe De Sena, CEO of Spartan Races (episode 58); Dr. John Nagl, a retired colonel and headmaster at the Haverford School for Boys (episode 36); and Dennis Boyle, co-founder of IDEO (episode 99). They had occasions to lean on their personal belief that honesty will reign supreme. Most guests' discussions around honesty were personal in nature and I found myself curious as to how honesty shows up in an organization, so I also turned to the academic literature.

A 2009 article by Daniel Palmer provides the framework for the role honesty plays in developing integrity in an organization.[1] Palmer describes three levels of ethical analysis that I use to describe three types of honesty relationships: transparent leader-follower relationships, colleague-to-colleague honesty and organizational culture driven by honesty and integrity. It got me thinking, how do authentic leaders engage in these different relationships?

The first honesty relationship is that involving leader-follower transparency. This relationship is based on building trust through knowledge sharing, where the leader displays high levels of openness, self-disclosure and trust in close relationships.[2] For an authentic leader, this is a critical skill for building trust and respect and for promoting the need for continuous honest feedback between you and your team.

If a CEO or leader exudes this trait, it will permeate the organization's culture. For example, there comes a time in every leader's tenure when it is necessary to resolve a situation with an employee who is not performing at a level the organization needs and who needs to be let go or transitioned into another role. Or the organization may be going through a tough period and needs to downsize. In either case, it is the leader's responsibility to have these difficult, but necessary, conversations.

However, fear holds most of us back from having difficult conversations. In these instances, you should ask yourself, "What would I want?" And since integrity is core to authentic leadership, the answer should be easy. In chapter 1, I shared Joe Burton's story about how he walked into the CEO's office and said he was quitting. Joe didn't dramatize the circumstances of his departure but rather focused on honest and transparent conversation. Transparent conversations between leader and follower demonstrate the power of openness between the various levels of an organization.

The second relationship is colleague-to-colleague. These relationships can be personal, and they typically have a give-and-take dynamic, although we've all worked with colleagues who only take, so that in return we feel taken advantage of. It is in these moments of honest personal conversation that an authentic leader's integrity is on full display. Authentic leaders thrive in these relationships, because they allow leaders to develop trust and set a tone in the organization that indicates that sharing, empathy and hopefully compassion (we'll get this in the next chapter) are part of the organization's fabric. Colleague-to-colleague honesty is demonstrated, for example, when a colleague shares with you that they are going through a divorce, bankruptcy or some other kind of personal crucible. It is in these moments that giving honest constructive feedback takes courage, as the feedback may not be what the other person wants to hear.

Brad Cooper, CEO of U.S. Corporate Wellness, uses the concept of colleague-to-colleague honesty when his organization works with employers around corporate wellness. U.S. Corporate Wellness partners with small to medium-size organizations to help create, support and build corporate health and wellness programs. Their point of differentiation is their personal health coaches. I asked Brad what makes his company unique compared to the competition. Here is what he said:

Our approach is to come in and literally create a *meaningful relationship between the employee and the coach that they are working with.* Supplement that with all the other components. Whereas [with] most wellness companies, it's the reverse. It's "Let's focus on all the other components, let's track your points, let's plug in your Fitbit, let's do the contest, let's plug in what you're doing on a daily basis or with your eating. And, oh, by the way, we have coaching." But the coaching is utilized similar to an EAP [employee assistance program], probably in the 3 percent to 5 percent range, whereas ours is in that 40 percent to 80 percent range, and then we supplement coaching with the other components. We all offer the same stuff, if you list it out in bullet points. Our main component is over here; the competition is over there. The competition has coaching— our main one, but we flip-flopped the emphasis. (Episode 60)

If you've ever had coaching, you know that a good coach will tell you the good, the bad and the ugly, all with the goal of making you a better person and supporting you on your journey. You can infer that since this is Brad's company, its corporate philosophy is an extension of Brad's core belief. And after an hour of conversation, I could see that it is. Brad is all about honesty and integrity.

The final honesty relationship is based on an organizational culture driven by honesty and integrity. This is developed, created and supported from the top down, and at each level of the organization there is an underlying drive to develop more leaders with higher levels of integrity (that is, more authentic leaders). Dr. Fred Kiel, author of *Return on Character: The Real Reasons Leaders and Their Companies Win*, was curious whether employees at eighty-four companies he studied perceived leadership to express the values of integrity, responsibility, compassion and forgiveness, and what impact that had on their return on assets (ROA). He found that organizations that were perceived to be strong across the four values had an average ROA of 9.3 percent. Those low on the four values managed to average an insignificant ROA of 1.93 percent.[3]

I wonder how leaders like the following would have come across in interviews. Over the last twenty years, several large organizations have been seen to lack even a modicum of honesty and transparency at the leadership level. In 2001, Enron and its accounting partner, Arthur Andersen (which was dissolved after the crisis), were found to have engaged in faulty accounting practices that led to hiding billions of dollars in debt and losses from bad deals and projects. At the time, this was the largest bankruptcy ever recorded. In 2014, General Motors recalled over 800,000 small cars due to a faulty ignition that resulted in 124 fatalities, and further recalls totaled 30 million vehicles globally. To make things worse, GM had known of the problem for over a decade. Whether we're talking about Volkswagen (fixing emission numbers), Mylan (increasing the cost of the EpiPen more than 500 percent over seven years), Enron or General Motors, they all had leaders who had questionable integrity that led to a culture of dishonesty.

A culture of dishonesty not only undercuts the notion of authentic leadership, it also creates a Machiavellian culture where only the strong survive while the weak get crushed. These are only a handful of well-known examples of leaders operating in a moral vacuum. You can dive into history and find leaders who were intoxicated by the scent of power or swayed by group-think. In either case, the ends never seem to quite justify the means in achieving organizational objectives.

100 Percent Honesty, 90 Percent of the Time

Lying, by Sam Harris, is a good starting point to gain a better understanding of the role of honesty and integrity.[4] It raises the question, Is an authentic leader honest 100 percent of the time? Probably not, so should a leader even be held to such a standard? According to Sam Harris, integrity is demonstrated when an individual's actions do not lead to or result in moments of shame and remorse and they have no need to lie about their personal life. Sam dives in particular into the idea of white lies. You know—those lies you tell because you are embellishing a story or trying to be kind and not hurt someone's feelings. For example, "The fish I caught was *this big*" (please put your hands up and pretend you caught a fish; now move them further apart). Or, the worst, "How does this dress make me look?" As a male, I'd rather have my teeth pulled out with no Novocain than answer that question.

As an authentic leader, you're faced with white lie moments all the time. What I love about the book *Lying*, and what it has to say about white lies in particular, is that Sam's philosophy is that he can't read minds (and therefore must avoid making assumptions): when asked a question, he will base his answer solely on the words that come out of the other person's mouth. Taking that premise, how can an authentic leader be 100 percent honest? It is never an easy task, and the right framing of the answer is a special skill, but if your colleague or subordinate asks you a direct question about their performance, the best course of action is to give them honest feedback.

As I've said before, ask yourself what response *you* would want if you asked someone the same question. You don't expect people to be brutal with their feedback but to be tactfully honest. Honest feedback can be the single most important bit of feedback a person gets. When I didn't receive tenure at my last job, a colleague told me that sometimes not getting the thing you want most works out best in the long run. There's a lot of truth in that bit of advice. It was one of my personal nudges.

In 1998, I worked for NAS. My boss was the regional VP and gave me some advice that I hold true to this day. I am paraphrasing, but he said, "If you hear a bit of feedback once, put a stake in the ground about the information. If you hear the same feedback a second time, reflect on it and consider if there is any truth to the information. But if you get the same feedback from a third person, it's true, so make a change." Since that nugget was delivered, I have always had my antennae up when it comes to receiving feedback.

Ego versus Fear: A Zero-Sum Game

When we look at leaders who lack integrity, we find two major culprits: ego and fear. Ego is your self-esteem or self-importance, and can be a force for evil when it comes to how far a person goes to positioning their strengths and weaknesses, especially in the face of not knowing how to do their job. If a leader has a bigger than average ego or sense of self-importance, they make decisions based on their belief that they either know the answer or can solve the problem. The question is, where does self-confidence leave off and become arrogance? Well, it's at the point where a person lacks the wisdom to know the difference. Without such wisdom, a leader is left with an acute degree of low self-awareness that can result in their ego writing checks that the organization can't cash, and scandal follows, which happened to the Enrons, GMs, Volkswagens and Mylans of the world.

On the other side of inflated self-importance are those who are ruled by fear. Fear is a universal emotion, as discussed in the previous chapter. It's so deeply rooted that it can be applied across all the contexts of authentic leadership. However, when it comes to integrity, fear can impact a leader's ability to do what is right, whether out of fear of disappointment, of losing their job or of retribution within the organization.

In chapter 2, I shared a story about Ron Wiens, who decided not to coach a leader because she ruled by fear and intimidation. When I asked Ron for his thoughts on why he believed the leader instilled a culture of fear, he told me it was simple: it is her fear of being seen as an impostor. This leader was making low-integrity choices because she thought that her colleagues would think that she was a fraud and that she was inept. In the end, Ron said, she managed from a place of low self-esteem.

Feeling "less than" because of a mistake or being judged can be crippling for many. But from an integrity standpoint, if you're high in authenticity, you're high in self-awareness. If you're high in self-awareness, then you're able to be honest with yourself and check your integrity level and moral compass to know what you should and should not do, and when you should speak up for the greater good of the organization.

Dr. Phil Said It, So It Must Be True: Behavior Integrity

Let me start with a quote from Dr. Phil: "The best predictor of future behavior is past behavior." I'm not an avid watcher of Dr. Phil, but this particular line has always resonated with me. It is with this line in mind that behavioral integrity came into focus during the interviews. Thus, I also sought out the work of Cornell University's Dr. Tony Simons, a globally recognized leader in the field of behavior integrity in the workplace. According to Dr. Simons, behavioral integrity is the "perceived pattern of alignment between an actor's words and deeds."[5] It is in these psychological contracts that trust is developed in the leader-follower relationship. However, Simons explains, leading with complete behavior integrity has two sources of complexity. First is the simple nature of business complexities. The goalposts move on a project due to circumstances changing on the ground, and at times conflicting priorities arise. Second is the potential for communication breakdown.[6]

Although circumstances do impact direction and communication can break down, it is another form of behavioral integrity that I want to focus on. How many of you have had encounters, professional or private, where somebody tells you they're going to do something and then doesn't complete the task? When you follow up with them, they provide a roster of reasons as to why the job didn't get done. For many of you, it's easy to accept the justification for missed meetings, project deadlines and so on because you do the same. One of my best friends lives in New York, and we often talk about the city's professional life. He's told me that when someone says to you "I'll call or text you to go grab a drink," don't hold your breath—the phrase is meaningless. Everyone knows it's code for "I'll see you when I see you." So that led me to ask him, "How do you trust someone?" He just kind of shrugged, and I kind of got sad.

Take a moment and reflect on a leader who has typically stuck to their word. How did this leader make you feel? Like they'll be honest and are someone to be trusted? Now take a moment and reflect on a leader who struggled to follow through, who always had an excuse as to why commitments were left on the table. What kind of relationship would you have with *this* leader? Finally, ask yourself, where do *you* fall along the spectrum? Could you be complicit in a lack of follow-through?

Over the past twenty years I have come across many well-intentioned individuals who have difficulties setting boundaries for fear of disappointing their colleagues and friends. It is human nature to not want to disappoint your peers, so saying "yes" all the time is easier than saying "no." The irony is that saying "yes" with no follow-through is worse than saying "no" at the outset. You end up letting your colleagues down and creating a potential vacuum of trust, at the minimum low expectations of follow-through.

What's more, authentic leaders who are exceptionally high in behavioral integrity are committed to creating and managing expectations within the organization. When expectations are managed and trust is developed, organizational culture thrives and allows the leader to have the difficult conversations. In either case, when an authentic leader creates and fosters behavioral integrity, expectations in the organization are cultivated and managed, horizontally and vertically. When an authentic leader's actions and behaviors are congruent, levels of trust, loyalty and engagement are raised.

The Whole—and Nothing But the Whole—Being

Bill George's final context for integrity is the wholeness of the individual. An authentic leader is driven to do right, both professionally and personally, which is essentially moral integrity. In an hour-long interview, it's difficult to get a complete sense of who is truly morally driven to do right and who is engaging in impression management. As I have noted, most individuals put on their best face when they're on the podcast, engaging in impression management, so that makes it difficult to ascertain who among the guests is "whole" in Bill George's sense.

From living in three religiously different countries—predominantly Christian, Buddhist and Islamic—I've learned that core moral values are, at the basic level, the same. Karissa Thacker, in her book *The Art of Authenticity*, perfectly describes moral integrity: "I use the metaphor of an active internal GPS system—'active' meaning we have to keep the GPS system turned on and attuned. Making a left turn too early could get you going in a direction you do not want to go, and finding a way to make a U-turn on certain highways can take a long time."[7]

Bill George points out that even the best leaders with the clearest goals and values have difficulty always maintaining a moral compass: "The world may have very different expectations for you and your leadership than you have for yourself. Regardless of whether you are leading a small team or are at the top of a powerful organization, you will be pressured by external forces to respond to their needs and seduced by the rewards for fulfilling those needs. It requires courage and resolve to resist the constant pressures and expectations confronting you and to take corrective action when necessary."[8] The way I interpret Thacker's and George's comments is that power can be kryptonite for authentic leaders: it clouds judgment, and it is those with moral fortitude and with trust from others who are best able to self-correct, usually sooner rather than later.

Three Leaders Who Lead with Integrity

Conversation specifically about the relationship between moral-
ity and leadership rarely occurred in my interviews, but the
subject did emerge through a combination of factors. These
include the consistency of answers, how interviewees believed
they are perceived by others, and how they described their
career and, most importantly, their family. As I turned through
the pages of transcripts, I asked myself two questions: First,
what does their path tell me about who they are as an individual?
Second, is there anything in the conversation that indicates to
me that their moral views defined their actions, both professionally and privately? Let's look for answers from Jeffery Hayzlett,
Dennis Boyle and Jennifer Benz.

Jeffrey Hayzlett, Chairman of C-Suite Networks (Episode 95)

Jeffery Hayzlett is a three-time *New York Times* bestseller and
former CMO of Kodak. Over his long and rich career, Jeffrey
has bought and sold over 250 companies, transactions totaling
roughly $25 billion. His current role at C-Suite Networks is to
create the most trusted network of business professionals for
business professionals. Jeffrey wears his South Dakota roots on
his sleeve, and he is one of the most authentic individuals you
will ever meet. He's also the podcast host of *All Business with Jeffery Hayzlett*, and while on my show he told the story of a guest
he once had. I think the story will give you a little insight into
Jeffrey's integrity:

JEFFREY HAYZLETT: I said [to this guest], "Listen, if you were here,
I'd punch you in the throat." And I said this on air, and I kept on in
there because the guy was just a total . . . I mean, what he said and
how he said it. He's the guy that was in a Goldman Sachs elevator,

overheard in Goldman Sachs' elevator. And he's a trader and he referred to women as "goats." As in bait for Jurassic Park's dinosaurs. And I said, "Dude, you have a daughter, right?"

SHOW GUEST: "Yeah."

JEFFREY: "Don't you have any remorse in saying that?"

SHOW GUEST: "Well, you don't understand. It's the industry."

JEFFREY: "No, no, no. You're the ... The industry is the people that make up the fricking industry, and you're saying that you're okay with your daughter being bait for other guys."

SHOW GUEST: "Well, not *my* daughter."

JEFFREY: "Well, wait ... Well, my daughter's better? It's okay if it's my daughter and not your daughter? Dude, if you were right here, I'd punch you in the throat, right now. You disgust me. You disgust me, and people like you."

Hayzlett is a great example of an authentic leader who relies on 99 percent honesty all the time. Is having high integrity something he developed over the years as his career accelerated, or has he always had this degree of integrity? I would hedge a guess that he has always been forthright and transparent, and has always lived by a moral code. I mean, he still takes collection up at church when he's in Sioux Falls. But what I love most about this conversation is that it provides a snapshot of Jeffrey's integrity. He could have just as easily not bothered to call his guest out. He could have laughed it off and politely provided affirmation for the behavior by not disputing it. Instead, he had the moral compass to stand up for his own values and let the person know that he took issue with his attitude to women.

Jennifer Benz, CEO of Benz Communication (Episode 30)

Benz Communication is a thriving human resource communications firm based in San Francisco. Jennifer Benz grew up taking care of horses and llamas on a farm in Colorado, which is a great way to discover a work ethic and learn patience, trust and compassion, and also behavioral and moral integrity. You have to show up or the animals won't. One of Jennifer's passions is volunteering. Jennifer explained why she sees volunteering as a high purpose:

JAMES: You're very passionate about this nonprofit side, and I think this is awesome. Tell me more about this and how you got involved in the space.

JENNIFER BENZ: Well, I initially got involved in the nonprofit world through the Taproot Foundation. That is an organization in the U.S. that helps professionals donate their skills to nonprofits through very strategic, high-impact pro bono projects. Taproot is just an amazing organization. My friend Aaron Hurst started that organization well over ten years ago. I was lucky enough, through a series of coincidences, to meet Aaron and get connected to the organization very, very early on and just was able to do some fun and exciting work to help build out some of the HR practices that they have and, really, got committed to the idea of doing pro bono work. This is something that's embedded in the legal profession, where everyone is expected to do pro bono work. I absolutely believe that all professionals should do pro bono work—it's such an incredible way to learn and to give back . . .

Then, about ten years ago, I took some time off from work—this is before I started my business—and traveled in Central America and Mexico. My first stop was Guatemala, and I just fell in love with the country down there. It's an incredible country, so much beauty, so much cultural diversity and so many problems too, of course, very consistent with the rest of Central America.

Right now, I'm on the board of an organization called WINGS that does family health, women's health and family planning work in Guatemala. They're working in the most rural populations to help women and men have access to birth control and just baseline family health services. It's incredible the impact that this organization has, what you can do with just a little bit of health education or a little bit of access to birth control and to cervical cancer testing and so forth. It's an incredible country and I've been very lucky to be involved with that organization.

JAMES: Do you see your role evolving in nonprofit or expanding to different areas, different countries, maybe?

JENNIFER: I am sure that, for the rest of my life, I'll be involved with nonprofits in some way. It's just become part of who I am and what I think my contribution can be. Whether it's in Guatemala or here in San Francisco, there are so many different organizations that do incredible work.

JAMES: Did you learn that sense of social justice from growing up?

JENNIFER: I think from growing up that I certainly learned a lot—like to work hard and to not take things for granted. My parents really pushed us to accomplish things and do things that we could be proud of. I think the exposure to the nonprofit sector that I got through Taproot and then living in Guatemala really just solidified that for me. We're so fortunate here in the U.S. to grow up in the places that we have and so have the opportunity to help folks who didn't have that situation. There are unlimited opportunities to do that. It's part of the reason that I love the work we do in employee benefits too, because health and financial security are just the baseline of any family being successful, and there is so much need for help.

Jennifer's drive to give back beyond her company is a fine example of an authentic leader modeling "Do as I say and do." You can also see how her parents are a significant influence on her sense of social justice and on her volunteerism. When Jennifer talks about this topic, you can hear her light up. The passion comes through in her voice. You can also bet that she uses that moral compass to lead the organization.

Dennis Boyle, Co-founder of IDEO (Episode 99)

IDEO is one of the largest and most distinguished product design firms in the world, with over seven hundred employees across nine offices around the world. It can be argued that IDEO gets credit for developing the concept of design thinking. This concept has revolutionized the way organizations attack innovation and creativity. Co-founder Dennis Boyle's integrity is firmly placed in his Midwestern upbringing. Dennis discussed his family and the role it played in his life with me:

JAMES: Going back to your siblings, who one by one came out to join you, your sister comes out there [she moved to California]. Do you think they came out because you led the way and they all followed from that? Or did they all fall in love with the place, and you just happened to be there?

DENNIS BOYLE: No, I think I kind of led the way. They'll all say that. But they... I just made it possible to come visit. And my sister knew I was here, knew I wasn't just moving out for space, with nobody around. And I had a good job offer. And that started it. She's very influential in the family... And then I'm trying to think of who was next. I think Brendan was next, because he came and got in the same Stanford [Product Design] program. Then... I got Brendan an internship out here in the summer —[it] was a place I worked, Spectra-Physics. Then I got my younger brother, Matt, an internship at another company that he still works for. This is twenty-five years later. And then I think by the time we had like three or four here, then the other ones could . . . I had a whole lot of people to come visit and see. And it just became natural for my other brother and sisters to find work and move here.

JAMES: Well, I think what's great, though, as you talk about it—I mean, there's clearly this sense of family for you, and the strength of the relationship. I always joke that when you have a big family like that, there's always the black sheep . . . I use my wife's family as the exception . . . She's one of five, and she has four brothers. And they all disgustingly love each other and never fight. And the boys go on a ski trip every year with each other. And it's almost nauseous how well they get along—and I say that tongue in cheek. It sounds like you're the same way with your family. Is that all the siblings, you guys get along?

DENNIS: Yes. I think there's been a few differences, but they're quite unusual. I take a big week—the boys' weekend that's in the summer with all my brothers, and we just add brothers-in-law, and we add friends. And that's usually twelve to fifteen guys at my cabin up in the Sierras. And that's been a neat tradition for a number of years. Yes, take my boys on a skip trip.

JAMES: That's awesome.

DENNIS: Having these annual traditions of gatherings or trips. I've been doing that for years. I've noticed that with friends. And they just stick. I take the boys . . . mountain biking in Moab, Utah, for years, or the ski trip up in the Lake Tahoe region around Christmas.

JAMES: Yes. I'm not close to either of my brothers, right? For various psychologically damaging reasons, probably. But I'm not close to any of my brothers. And I always wonder what it's like to be close to your siblings. Like you do these ritualistic trips every year. Is it something you look forward to because you guys can be or act different, or be unique or create your own experiences? And those experiences feed you for another 365 days a year? What is it about this that kind of keeps you going every year?

DENNIS: Well, I'd have to say that it's sort of a reflection of a good childhood and a good experience growing up ... Our parents did this, would have these wonderful trips as family to a cottage on the lake. And we would just go up there and live and be with each other. My dad would drive twenty miles into work instead of one block to work but still worked. That just sort of established [a pattern]. And we did trips ... around the area, winter and summer to Detroit or some smaller trips to colleges for football games or something. It's a big family, so it's not that easy to move around ... Having these traditions of going to Howard Johnson's or staying at some place in Marshall, Michigan, or having these big family reunions every few years on my mother's side and my father's side (I have fifty-six first cousins) ... That tradition continues.

Like Jennifer, Dennis can attribute his integrity to his upbringing in the Midwest. With his integrity developed through his parents and community, Dennis was able to help grow IDEO and lead it to become the industry standard for design firms.

What Do These Stories Have in Common?

Jennifer Benz, Dennis Boyle and Jeffery Hayzlett all run organizations by example. Their commitment to their word came across very clearly in their interviews. Each of them was also very passionate about their family and the role they play in their family. Jennifer and Dennis emulated their upbringing, whereas Jeffrey was focused on *not* emulating his. Further, it was clear that the only way they could grow as people and influence the organization was by having a high level of transparency that enables them to be open and honest. It allows them to ask questions like "Are we doing the right thing?" or "Are we going the right direction?"

The Personal Integrity Conundrum

When I was about 13 or 14, I showed up at the house of a close family friend (I basically lived there during the summers) and, as my surrogate mom tells the story, I walked into their house and proclaimed that I was done lying. I don't know where this proclamation came from; perhaps at that moment I felt that I was being lied to or manipulated at home. I just know that from that day forward, when I was asked a question, it was hard not to give a truthful answer. It's not that I never lied again—I was a teenager and I wanted to have a sense of freedom. But if my parents asked me a question and I lied, it was written all over my face. I would get a knot in my stomach and my face would get hot.

I had a job in high school, and I recall that I called my boss at the Oregon Zoo to tell him I was sick and couldn't come to work (a good example of teenage dishonesty). Hold your applause—it was not that riveting a job: it was in food services, but it was perfect for a high school student. I believe I told my parents that my boss had called to tell me I didn't have to go in that day because it wasn't that busy at the zoo. Can you remember when you skipped school and knew the school was going to call and if you got to the phone first no one would be any wiser? Yeah, my boss didn't totally believe me and called my house later to test my sick theory. My mom suddenly became a lot wiser. What's interesting is what ensued. Doing what moms do, she thought she was protecting me by lying to my boss and saying I was sick. But when she got off the phone, she laid into me. I'm not sure if I said what I did next was because I wanted to be right or to justify my behavior, but in any case my response was, "I never asked you to lie for me." What was even more surprising is that my dad said, "He's right."

The point of the story is this: even at a young age, even if my moral (or honest) compass was still being forged, accountability prevailed for me. As I have matured (only slightly) and procreated (often), the idea of honesty and behavioral integrity has only become more pronounced. I even struggle to discuss Santa Claus, the Easter Bunny or the Tooth Fairy with my kids. It's super exhausting!

Final Thoughts (for Now) on Integrity

One of the central themes of the book is the role that a crucible plays in creating opportunities for individuals to become more self-aware. Authentic leaders assess their strengths and weaknesses and then decide where to focus their energy for improvement. Integrity is a slightly different animal in relation to the crucible, when considered in the context of what interviewees had to say about integrity. Most leaders' integrity was informed by their parents and the environment they were raised in.

Overall, what I found is that authentic leaders who are high in integrity fall into two camps. In the first camp are those individuals who had a crucible and are attuned to it, and who, aiming to be different and to live a life born out of their crucible, act with integrity. In the second camp are those individuals whose crucibles were not necessarily personal, but rather professional yet who remain positively impacted by a childhood environment that taught them how a life of integrity is meant to be lived.

Finally, the concept of integrity started off in this book for me as honesty. Honesty is something that I hold dear, and I expect those who are leading others to espouse this value, but as I developed this chapter and went through the interviews, it became clear that while honesty is an important attribute, it falls short as a predictor of authentic leadership. For example, take a leader who consistently fails to follow through. That leader can own it and admit to missing the deadline, but eventually their behavioral integrity will be questioned. It's clear that most leaders have integrity, but the question is, to what degree? Is integrity ever sacrificed to professional or personal gain?

Practicing Your Authentic Integrity

Here again I turned to Dr. Seth Gillihan and Dr. Kara O'Leary to help me create action activities that will help you grow your integrity. These are things you can do once, as they come or never. But if you choose "never," that won't really help you grow now, will it?

1. *Fine is okay, but...* When someone you care about asks how you're doing, give a truthful answer. You might be tempted to give the standard "fine" or "great!" even when you're not feeling fine or great. Take a moment to sense how you are and then let the person know—truthfully. This may feel awkward at first, but the reality is that we all have good days and bad days. Be aware of and acknowledge the differences.

2. *Share the impact.* Make a list of two or three individuals in your life who have had the greatest impact on your personal integrity. Then let them know how and why they affected you and how and why you appreciate them. For bonus points, look for several professional relationships in which you found the other person's integrity actions inspiring and motivating.

3. *Don't say yes for yes's sake.* Look for an opportunity today to

be more direct about how you think and feel. For example, if a colleague at work asks for your help on a project but you know you don't have the time, let your colleague know, perhaps with a proviso that you might have a window in due course. In this moment you have an opportunity to give feedback about the limitations you have and express any concerns that may arise.

4. *Sharing is caring.* Share more of yourself with someone you know than you otherwise might be inclined to. Be more open about your life, what's most important to you, your faith or spirituality, your fears and insecurities. Let others see you— the *real* you. This is scary, because it looks fear right in the eye. Remember, don't let fear conquer you—conquer your fear. One side note here: how the other person reacts is on them, not on what you say.

5. *Lead by example.* Being a leader means setting an example. Be honest when there is something to gain and someone to touch. Share hard truths when necessary, but in a kind way.

6. *Have the hard talk.* When you have to have a difficult conversation, think of it as an opportunity to be authentic and real with someone else. For example, if you're pleased with a certain co-worker's results, then share this, and be specific about what it is you like. Providing honest feedback (either positive or negative) builds bonds, nurtures trust and fosters loyalty. We all appreciate when someone notices.

Where Are We Going Next?

So far on this journey we have explored the impact of a leader's crucible in terms of providing the opportunity to change their self-awareness. When choosing to learn more about themselves, a leader can evaluate their strengths and weaknesses and make conscious decisions about how they want to evolve as a leader. This chapter has discussed the impact integrity can have both morally and behaviorally on a leader and those around that leader, and, in the end, on the organization. Thus, we make an addition to the authentic leadership equation, by adding integrity (I) to the model.

$$\text{Crucible} = (\Delta SA) + (\Delta I) = \text{Authentic Leadership}$$

Now the model indicates that the impact of a leader's crucible provides the opportunity for the leader to change their self-awareness and integrity (behavioral and moral), resulting in a more authentic leader. However, there is another piece the equation that needs to be discussed. As previously noted, a leader has an opportunity to lead by compassion. It is when an authentic leader begins to create moments of self- and other-focused compassion that the model of authentic leadership is further enhanced. The next chapter, therefore, explores the concept of compassion.

(4)

COMPASSION

LEAD FROM THE HEART

I believe that the methods by which we increase our altruism, our sense of caring for others and developing the attitude that our own individual concerns are less important than those of others, are common to all major religious traditions ... They all advocate love, compassion and forgiveness.

THE DALAI LAMA[1]

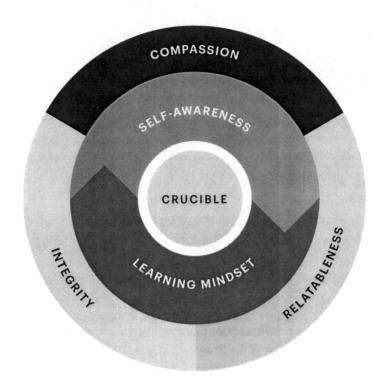

Let's Define Compassion

In his book *Wisdom: From Philosophy to Neuroscience,* Stephen Hall suggests that compassion is made up of three components. The first component is acknowledgment of and respect for another's perspective. This is really about possessing a heightened sense of emotional intelligence in order to better read cues from people around you. The second component requires a person to feel *something* in the "heart" of another person's pain, and this includes physical, emotional and mental pain. This is empathy. The third component is possessing an emotional response to another's suffering to such a degree that you must act. The action you take is a function of something personal to the you but also external. Thus, the compassionate authentic leader is motivated to reduce their own suffering as well as the suffering of others.[2]

Monica Worline and Jane Dutton, in *Awakening Compassion at Work*, suggest that compassion has a fourth component. We seldom consider that suffering occurs within organizations, that organizations could be that "human." But suffering *is* present, and it allows for the growth of an organizational culture of compassion. Compassion is different from exhibiting kindness, gratitude and happiness. Kindness is a desire to help someone flourish; happiness is a personal sense of well-being; and gratitude is a feeling of appreciation for experiences in one's life.[3] Worline and Dutton have written an excellent resource for those of you who want dive deep into compassion at work, at both leadership and organizational levels. Their work has informed my view of the role compassion plays in authentic leadership.

Organizational Culture and Suffering

In how a leader responds to suffering we can distinguish empathy from compassion. Empathy is the ability to understand the way someone is feeling in a given circumstance, likely because the empathetic person has had a similar experience. Yet an individual who feels empathy may not be compelled to relieve another person's suffering. In an organization, suffering comes in many different forms, from lack of respect for colleagues to pressure to meet unrealistic deadlines to failure to value accomplishments. However, we tend to associate suffering with tragedy or other serious life events—the death of a loved one, a divorce, being laid off and similar experiences.

Though these associations are accurate, suffering is also an intensely personal experience and will impact all of us differently.

A compassionate leader or colleague will not only feel empathy, but will intrinsically feel compelled to help diminish the suffering of the other person. This does not necessarily mean doing that person's work, but it could be expressed in the form of a simple act of kindness that can create momentary relief.

Let's explore suffering during an organizational downsizing. Downsizing is a highly stressful experience for all involved. If you are among those being made redundant (the politically correct word for being laid off or fired), you will feel rejected, sad, stressed about what to do next and very likely concerned about how you're going to pay the bills. If you are the leader accountable for ensuring that the downsizing goes to plan, you may feel guilt, shame and stress because of the impact you're seeing on those who are leaving the company. The people who are left behind will likely feel guilt, as they have kept their jobs while their colleagues have been let go. Through and through, this is a crappy situation.

As I noted, I have been made redundant. At my previous academic job, I didn't get tenure. For those who aren't familiar with the tenure process, it's higher education's version of a job for life. Essentially, you make your case to a group of your peers that you are contributing value to the institution by being an effective teacher and producing research, and thus providing a service to the academic community at large.

My peers decided that I was not contributing enough research, so I was axed. I had known I would be on the fence for tenure, but I'd felt that I had accomplished enough to secure permanent residence. So when the call came that I didn't get tenure, I was sad and felt rejection and shame. In an aim to relieve my suffering, the provost (the academic CEO) and the dean offered to help and let me teach a summer course so that I had health insurance for my family. They understood that with four kids to feed, I needed a little stability.

A Business Case for Compassion in the Workplace

I can imagine that the thought of expressing compassion in the workplace makes some of you feel a bit awkward, maybe even uncomfortable, and that you might think that compassion in a leader is a sign of weakness. When I began to write this chapter, the theme I set out to explore was how empathy is unequivocally an attribute of authentic leadership. But as I dug in and started culling the transcripts and research, it became clear that empathy is a baseline and that it's compassion that is the higher expression in authentic leadership. Compassion is a hard virtue to achieve, because it requires putting aside one's ego and putting others first.[4]

Lee Cockerell, former executive vice president of operations for Walt Disney World Resort, had a hard upbringing. His crucible both created opportunities and, at times, limited his professional development. Like most authentic leaders I interviewed, Lee evolved, grew and learned to embrace his past as an opportunity to innovate leadership inside Disney. As a guest on *Executives After Hours*, he suggested that "with discipline and compassion, you can go a long way" (episode 115). Discipline, for him, was about showing up and following through, or behavioral integrity.

Lee also used the word *compassion*, and to a degree it surprised me, as most leaders don't overtly use that word, and if they do, they tend to use it interchangeably with *empathy*. However, when I dug a little deeper for an explanation of what Lee meant by compassion, he said that he felt compelled to help others in good and bad times—that is, to relieve suffering. Lee gives credit for his success to his past, his mistakes and his persistence, all of which helped develop his compassionate leadership.

So, how might compassion impact the workplace? Kim Cameron, David Bright and Arran Caza investigated eighteen organizations (with 804 respondents) to determine if perceived virtuousness, of which compassion is one aspect, impacts organizational behavior as well as financial and organizational performance.[5] Their findings were published in *American Behavioral Scientist*. What they found is a significant relationship between perceived virtuousness in organizational behavior and perceived performance. When employees believe that their organization is acting virtuously, they perceive that the organization is better performing. However, we all know that perception is often different from reality, so the researchers took a deeper look at the proposed relationship between virtuousness and performance. They investigated twelve publicly traded companies, conducted a hierarchal linear regression and found that, statistically, companies that perceived their organization as having high levels of virtuousness had significantly higher profits. This is a very small sample, but telling.

When organizations foster compassion, then, there is at least tangential evidence that there is a return on investment (ROI). Taking this a step further, reflect on a time when someone showed *you* compassion. How did you respond? Were you more thankful? Was trust increased between you and the other person? If it was a leader or colleague, were you willing to work harder for that individual? In other words, the aim of this string of questions is to wonder out loud if the intangible benefits of practicing organizational compassion equal or outweigh the financial impact.

The Role of Self-Compassion in Leadership

One of the themes that sprang up at me while trawling through the interviews looking for examples of compassion is this notion of self-compassion and leaders' success. As I noted in the introduction, this book (and thus the podcast) started out as a wellness book for CEOs, so over my first seventy interviews, I asked my guests how they defined wellness. The responses varied, but there was an overwhelming theme of self-care or self-compassion, both psychological and physical. Dr. Seth Gillihan (episode 9) and Dr. Kara O'Leary (episode 46) provide two great examples of defining wellness with a focus on self-compassion. Seth said, "Actually, I would define wellness as being able to recognize and meet our needs in ways that are consistent with our values," whereas Kara defined wellness "in a kind of a balanced, holistic way, I would say. So, I would think of wellness in terms of psychological health probably first and foremost, and then in terms of physical health and creating space in one's life to sort of nurture those different aspects. So, both the mental and the physical."

Both of these definitions reflect the concept of self-compassion. Leaders who understand the importance of self-compassion and try to put it into practice in their daily life have a much more balanced approach to success and failure. Laura Putnam, CEO of Motion Infusion and bestselling author of *Workplace Wellness That Works*, who was a guest on my show, defines wellness in a compassionate way:

I really define it as a medium to allow human beings to be human beings. As human beings—and this is more on a physical level—we are designed to move. A lot of this is kind of closing in on what I like to call the "cultural biological mismatch." We're culturally mandated to sit, but we're biologically programmed to move. Also, as human beings, we're designed to eat healthy foods. We're designed to take breaks. We're hardwired to be social. We each have an innate desire to become our best selves and reach our full potential. We all want to make the world a better place. That, to me, is really the essence of being human. That, to me, is what wellness or well-being or even health, whatever you want to call it, is. Really, at its best, that's what it's designed to do. (Episode 23)

Laura strives to educate people and organizations to be more compassionate towards themselves. This leads to being compassionate to others. Dr. Joel Bennett, CEO of Organizational Wellness & Learning Systems, says similar things about self-compassion:

It's really important when you ask, where does resilience fit into this? I'm so happy you mentioned compassion because a lot people, when they talk about resilience, talk about the commitment and confidence, and the centering aspects of resilience—commitment being "I'm going to get through this." Persevering, goal setting, making things happen. Confidence being "I can get through this. I have the ability to do so. I have the self-efficacy, the internal locus of control, to do this." Centering being whether it's your mindfulness-based skills you're using, or acceptance and commitment skills, whatever you're having to use. (Episode 13)

Finally, Greg Zlevor, founder & CEO of Westwood International and a genuinely kind individual, talked about what happened to him when he lost sight of self-compassion. When Greg and I spoke, we dove into the negative consequences of pleasing others at the cost of hurting yourself. Greg shared with me a relationship that had gone astray and compromised his core being, and how if he had just been more self-compassionate, things would have ended a bit differently. Here are Greg's words, about how lack of self-compassion leads to:

Having a difficulty or a tension in a relationship instead of doing what is really best. I was in a recent relationship where my spirituality was ridiculed—subtly, but ridiculed and certainly not supported. So I gave up parts of it so it wouldn't cause tension. As I'm looking back on it, trying to please was really not doing a service to the world. I could have stood up for myself in a more compassionate and clear way. It still would have allowed the other people to save face and their opinion on what they wanted to do, and [allowed] me still do what I needed to do. (Episode 94)

For Laura, Joel, Greg, Seth and Kara, self-compassion is a critical part of their identity, and one that helps each of them be a better human being. They practice mindfulness, resilience and self-compassion to be better leaders. I found that when individuals neglect self-compassion, they suffer. When they suffer, they begin to compromise their own self and become embroiled in their own problems, resulting in being a little less authentic and diminished as a present leader.

The Power of Compassion

Leaders who practice self-compassion, I discovered, can move mountains when it comes to leading. Mark Crowley, who I've referenced in previous chapters, wrote the book *Lead from the Heart*. Mark is a servant leader, and he leads in a way to empower his colleagues to be the best human beings they can be. He starts by caring about them, asking questions about how things are going and finding a way to help those around him succeed. Mark is a compassionate leader; he creates a culture that is caring, engaged and loyal to the mission and values he espouses. It is these intangibles that I think are sacrificed to quarterly reports to investors. Often we hear rumblings like "We didn't make our numbers for this quarter, so let's work harder, longer and scrap the current strategy." In the end, employees burn out faster and are less happy, and the organization can separate from its core.

The point I am trying to make is that when authentic leaders summon up compassion for their colleagues' challenges, no matter how big or small, they are actually empowering the *organization* to do great things. By the way, having compassion does not equal being weak in any way. Compassion enables effective communication and can optimize an authentic leader's relationships with colleagues.[6]

For me, sharing my own story is an important aspect of the podcast interviews. The aim (besides having minimal shame) is to make a personal connection with my guests and make them feel comfortable enough to share their stories. Thus, I listen carefully from a place of compassion, which impacts the dynamic I have with many guests and builds rapport. So when I think across the interviews I have conducted, what I love most is the times when leaders engage in honest and passionate conversations that result in transparent discussions, often touching on compassion. And this got me thinking that if these authentic leaders are sharing their "dirty laundry" with *me* about their past, what kind of social impact are they having in their organization? Let's look at three authentic leaders who opened up about compassion.

Three Stories of Compassionate Authentic Leaders

I think of compassion as the top of a pyramid. Leaders who demonstrate compassion tend to practice both self- and external compassion, and though I could have selected any number of leaders who demonstrate this quality, the Reverend Richard Pengelley, Dr. Michelle Robin and Mitch Martin are the first who came to mind. These three, whether on the podcast or in life, have an internal drive to help others. Through their own suffering they are able to understand others' suffering, and embracing compassion helps them in their authentic leadership. Let's start with my conversation with Richard.

The Very Reverend Richard Pengelley, dean of Perth's Anglican Diocese: "The Journey to the Soul" (Episode 33)

The Very Reverend Richard Pengelley is a two-time Olympian and dean of the Perth, Australia chapter of the Anglican Church. Reverend Pengelley and I had a wide-ranging conversation about a dad who was demanding, a sport that created opportunities and a faith that drove him towards a life of compassion. I think it would be safe to suggest that one source of Richard's compassion is the Bible, but what I think goes unsaid in my interview with him is the impact his dad had on his compassion. He describes his dad as cold, distant, hard and a control freak, but a devout Anglican. He describes his mother as the rock in the family:

From a very early age, I remember intimacy, and as a small child, but then almost literally being pushed away as I got to sort of 7, 8, 9 years of age, to toughen up and be a man. Again, a very traditional model.

Richard went on to describe tremendous acceptance of a difficult situation for any child and coming to terms with his emotional and physical connection with his own children. Later in the interview we talked about our dads passing away and he shared a forgiving and tender moment with his dad:

I'll tell you one story. I mentioned previously that sort of coming into his chest, hairy chest, running my little toy cars up and down his chest and being very tender, but then feeling pushed away. "It's time to become a man," and that was his motto. From that point on, the most physical contact we had, he used to shake my little finger when he congratulated me for a fine sporting performance. So, little finger to little finger is about as little contact that you can have with a human being.

I took him his final Eucharistic Communion, the day before he died. So as a priest, I took him Mass Communion. After I anointed him on the forehead with the holy oil, he took my thumb and kissed it and to me—that was a profound moment of seeing him healing.

Richard and I discussed the role his dad played, but what matters most here is Richard's ability to forgive and almost embrace his dad for his strengths and weaknesses—something that many of us struggle with in regard to our parents. In the end, the Reverend Pengelley was called to lead compassionately.

Mitch Martens: Cedars-Sinai's Compassion Wingman (Episode 66)

Mitch Martens is the employee wellness administrator at Cedars-Sinai Medical Center and is responsible for managing roughly twenty thousand employees' health and wellness (full-time, part-time and contract workers). His job is to live and breathe strategies and tactics for how to get employees to be more compassionate towards themselves and others. In the interview, one thing that came out about Cedars-Sinai, clearly driven by Mitch, is that Cedars-Sinai meets its employees at the exact point they need to along their life journey. Essentially, Cedars-Sinai wants to relieve employees' suffering, thus acting compassionately. But where does Mitch get his drive to be compassionate? I think it comes from his family. When Mitch came out as gay, he was not sure how his family would respond. I'll let Mitch tell you how his mother reacted:

JAMES: So when you came out to your family, what was that situation like? I mean that's pretty personal, but...

MITCH MARTENS: Wow no, I love it. I love that question, and I love talking about it. I came out to each one of them individually at different times. The first one was my mother, and ironically, it was while... I had to go back and live at home. I mean, I'm a senior in college. What does that make me—19, 20, I don't know, 21?

JAMES: Twenty-one, 22, yeah.

MITCH: It's like you *know* I'm just going nuts. Partly I'm in pain because of this brachial plexus issue, and it's like two in the morning and I'm debating, "Do I tell her? Do I finally tell her? Is this the time?" Like a stupid 5-year-old, I go and knock on her door at two in the morning and I'm like, "Mom, are you awake?" Immediately she sits up, like any instinctual mother, like, "Oh my God, there's something wrong with my child." She's like, "Of course I am. What's wrong? What's wrong?"

I just kind of looked at her and was like, "I don't feel well." I mean, I swear to God, it's amazing how I reverted back to being like a 5-year-old. She sits me down on the bed and she's like, "Well, what's going on?" I'm like, "I don't know," and because she's such an instinctual, wonderful mother, I will never, ever forget what she said to me. Oh God, it still makes me emotional. She said to me, she goes, "Mitch, tell me something. Does your tummy hurt, or does your heart hurt?"

At that moment, I knew. I knew that it was okay to talk to her, and I told her, and she had been waiting for a long time and she could get it. She said, "Mitch, I'm not surprised." She goes, "I never knew, was I supposed to approach you about it? Should I wait until *you* approach *me* about it?" She goes, "I'm so glad we can talk about this."

She actually said, she goes, "You know, I've never had a child in this situation. I don't know how to deal with this. Do you want to go to therapy? Not because I think there's something wrong with you, but I don't know how to help you and I know you're struggling." She goes, "No parent ever wants to see their child struggle."

In this instance, Mitch's compassion was formed, fostered and became a core motivator in his leadership style. This is why his work at Cedars-Sinai is a perfect fit for his skills, and I would even say compassion is his superpower. Later in the interview, I asked Mitch to share with me how Cedars-Sinai practices compassion. Here are some insights:

JAMES: Yeah, so it seems to me like the big takeaway I'm getting is that after the two-day seminar where they figure out what their personal [goal is], what they want . . . What you try to do as an organization is show them all the tools that are there and leave it to them to engage in those tools.

MITCH: Right. And those tools can be not just lying out there in front of them, but they can call us, and again, using the analogy, they can say, "You know, I want to know how to use that hammer." "Great, we'll stand with you and show you how to hammer," as opposed to "Here's a hammer. Go do something with it."

It's more than just realizing the tools are there. It's also realizing that we will partner with you. We will be a journeyman. We will be a shepherd and walk with you if you want us on your path. Call us when you want us, and when you don't want us, that's okay, but I want you to know that we are here when you're ready to have us on your journey. Whether that's for five minutes or five years, we're here.

Mitch's journey to become more compassionate, like many, happened when he least expected it. It was Mitch coming out as gay that put him on a new path of compassionate living, and in turn inspired Mitch to create systems for employees at Cedars-Sinai that reflect that compassion.

Dr. Michelle Robin: Putting the "S" in Self-Compassion (Episode 55)

Dr. Michelle Robin is the chief wellness officer and founder of The Wellness Connection, just outside Kansas City, Kansas. Michelle has been a practicing chiropractor for twenty-four years. Like many leaders I interviewed, Michelle has experienced some trials and tribulations in her life. During our conversation, she talked about how humans are creatures of habit, and how her mom, she felt, was no different. She said that her mom was married four times, and that opened the door to asking if Michelle saw any patterns with her mom:

JAMES: From your mom, I think there's a couple things. I think about people I know whose parents have been married multiple times. I feel like you have a couple directions you can go when it comes to the moment of reckoning. What lessons did you learn from your mom's patterns?

MICHELLE ROBIN: That's a great question. I think I have learned about self-care. I had to learn compassion. For the first thirty-one years of my life, I was pushing to be valued and loved by somebody outside of myself. I had a big old wake-up call at 31 and had the outside success, but did not have the inside piece. I had spent the last almost nineteen years working on the inside piece and how could I really love me and be okay with Michelle Robin? And what am I here to do on the planet? How can I show up?

I'm a fairly positive person by nature. Sometimes I get coined as a Pollyanna. It doesn't mean I don't have fears. I'm actually a fear-based personality. I just push through it by some of the tools I use. I think [my mom] really just laid the groundwork for me to have compassion for other people. If you come in to see me [at her practice], James, I'll do a detailed history and I'll ask, "Tell me about your life, James." Or "Were you a vaginal birth or C-section birth?" That matters in health and wellness. Or "Were your parents married, divorced? Did you move a lot as a kid? Did you have any broken bones, stitches, surgeries, marriages, kids, etc.?"

I go through that to get a picture of your life, to get a snapshot. If you're going to give me the most important asset you own to give you guidance on, your well-being, I need to know you more. I know some patients are like, "Oh my God, I can't believe your paperwork," or "Why do you care? Can't you just give me a pop-and-go experience?"

JAMES: For your mom—because I don't want to go off this topic because I think it's a really important topic to talk about . . . it sounds like *you* learned the sense of compassion, but how did you learn that compassion [from your mom]? Do you know what I mean? I feel like you have this really outgoing, bubbly personality, very magnetic. Some individuals who don't would have a detachment disorder. Some that have it are going to gravitate towards whoever will love them.

It sounds like when you described it, that's kind of what you were going through in your twenties is that pattern. I'm trying to figure out, then, where does that compassion you learned from your mom come from? What compassion?

MICHELLE: I think that as I can look back on my life, my mother taught me compassion all along because as a kid we always were taking people in. We were the type of family that if we met you at the grocery store and we were having dinner that night and you do not have any place to go, we would invite you, or my mother would invite you. I wouldn't. I personally, at that age—our house was crazy. I didn't want to have any more people in there. "Have open arms." My mother taught me that.

I think that I had some resentment towards her for possibly feeling like she was choosing men over her children. I had to work on that. Your parents do the best job they can with the tools they have.

Michelle's story is a great reminder for leaders who tend to carry their past in their back pocket. Too often in times of stress, discomfort and uneasiness, the first place we go emotionally and mentally is our childhood. What Michelle is suggesting is that by first loving yourself and practicing self-compassion, you have the ability to increase your compassion for others—and thus, to lead from a position of compassion.

What Do These Leaders Have in Common?

Compassion is hard. To be compassionate means that you need to have an internal drive to relieve another person's suffering. Reverend Pengelley, Mitch and Michelle all had a point in their life when they were suffering and felt the relief of the suffering when people around them helped them in their moment of need. All three interviewees had formal training and, today, espouse these values. In addition, they use the ability to be compassionate as a means to build significant and meaningful relationships. Mitch uses his crucible as the jumping-off point to compassionate living, but this happened only after those close to him helped relieve *his* suffering. Many authentic leaders grow into this notion of compassion by practicing compassion and, more importantly, having compassionate moments when they are in need.

What Role Does Compassion Play in My Life?

Of all the themes in this book, this is actually, for me, the hardest to articulate in terms of self-reflection and personal growth. I look at my experience with compassion in two ways. I look at the personal compassion, meaning my family, and I look at external compassion, meaning relationships that might or might not be close.

I have a tendency to empathize with people who I don't have a deep personal relationship with. On the surface, this may not make a lot of sense. Let me explain. There are individuals I was close to who created a cycle of personal sabotage for themselves, and who in that cycle have struggled to make fundamental changes that would allow them some happiness. With these individuals, over time, I have moved from compassion to frustration, ultimately landing on indifference. Empathy got choked off.

But the more deeply I became involved in this book, and the more I read and researched, and the more I interviewed people who are highly compassionate, the more I came to see the benefits they have in their life through their compassion. What is really interesting when you read about compassion, for example, is the process called *compassion fatigue*. People who are highly compassionate actually exhaust themselves, because they take on the burden of so many people's emotions and feelings in trying to relieve the suffering of others. I'm not saying that's why I'm not compassionate, because I don't want to experience compassion fatigue. That would be a bullshit excuse. I'm saying that I have compassion to a point, but maybe not as much as I should. At the end of the day, for me, compassion is an ongoing journey, and I'm sure I'll be more compassionate in twenty years than I am now. At least I sure hope so.

Final Thoughts (for Now) on Compassion

Compassion is a difficult concept for leaders, because it can be perceived as a weakness or liability. How do you manage people from not taking advantage of your compassion? Is there a line you can cross to where compassion is not respected? Some literature states that compassion is a force for good and not only helps the financial bottom line, but also helps an organization's culture. When an authentic leader espouses compassionate values and creates shared experience across the organization, that leader is able to move mountains and create healthy communities that thrive.

Monica Worline and Jane Dutton offer a great starting point to deepen your knowledge around compassion. Beside addressing the role suffering plays and the direct role of a leader in mitigating suffering, they make a great case for suffering as creating meaningful shared experiences. These experiences are what build trust, respect, engagement, loyalty and productivity in the workplace. However, and what may be most important, they also believe, as I do, that compassion can be taught. It is a learnable skill that is increased by practicing.

Practicing Compassion

Author Elizabeth Pybus describes the simplicity and the complexity of being compassionate: "Compassion cannot be imposed on us from outside. It is something freely given from within. Both the freedom and the innerness of compassion as a response are essential elements in compassion which make us value it."[7] This may remind you of the difficulties change creates in general, and compassion creates specifically, in that we all have change or compassion inside us but unless we are intrinsically motivated to be more compassionate, be more self-aware or increase our integrity, change will be only temporary.

Once again, I turn to my good friends Dr. Seth Gillihan and Dr. Kara O'Leary for their expertise on how *you* can work towards being a more compassionate leader, and thus just a little more authentic.

1. *Practice compassionate meditation.* Drs. Gillihan and O'Leary recommend that you make time to practice a loving-kindness meditation in which you focus on self-compassion as well as other-focused compassion. Dr. O'Leary suggests that you

take a few minutes each day to recognize all of the stressors you are managing and to cultivate appreciation and compassion for this experience. This practice can help cultivate well-being through less extreme reactions to life events and less rumination about misgivings.

Note: UC Berkeley's Greater Good Science Center, in collaboration with HopeLab, launched Greater Good in Action, which synthesizes all the best research and practices and provides great examples of how to practice compassion. The Greater Good in Action website can guide you on your compassionate meditation: ggia.berkeley.edu/practice/loving_kindness_meditation. You can also check out this site: soundcloud.com/hachetteaudiouk/meditation-seven-befriending.

2. *Listen empathically.* This is the art of listening to your colleagues or family with intent. This is a skill that requires you not to worry about trying to fix someone's problem and asks you to be present, listen with intent and refrain from judging. To practice this, turn off your email, silence your phone and move yourself to a space free of distractions. This not only ensures your focus will be directed to the other person, but lets the other person know that you care. They are more likely to open their hearts and be more open and present.

3. *Be the ray of sunshine.* Have you had one of those days, weeks, months or years where all you needed to get you through the day was a hug or a thoughtful text message? Take a minute and think of someone around you who is going through a difficult time and send them a handwritten note or text message, or go get them a coffee. Try to make this a weekly habit—you will be amazed at the boomerang effect.

4. *Fix a stranger's flat tire.* Take the opportunity to open the door for someone carrying boxes or give up your seat on the bus to

a person who needs it. When I lived in Japan, it was common to see men and women get up and give their seat to someone who was older or to a pregnant woman (regardless of age). It is these little gestures that remind you and those around you of humanity and our need to have more compassion for those who may be in need.

5. *Put the gavel down.* Look for an opportunity to go easy on someone who would be easy to judge (such as the slow driver who is inconveniencing you). Think about times you've been cut a break and see if you can cut someone else some slack. We never know what events are happening in others' lives, so try starting from the position that "they could be having a bad day." This can help you practice forgiveness.

6. *Volunteer.* I don't really need to elaborate here. It's good for your soul, it helps those who need it and it can remind you to be thankful for what you have, not focused on what you don't have.

Where Do We Go from Here?

So far on this journey we have explored the impact of a leader's crucible in terms of providing the opportunity to change their self-awareness. When learning more about themselves, a leader can change the role of integrity in the workplace. This chapter discussed the impact of self and other compassion can have on leaders and those around them. Thus, we make an addition to the authentic leadership equation by adding compassion (C) to the model:

$$\text{Crucible} = (\Delta \text{SA}) + (\Delta \text{I} + \Delta \text{C}) = \text{Authentic Leadership}$$

Now the model indicates that the impact of a leader's crucible provides the opportunity for the leader to change their self-awareness, integrity and compassion, resulting in a more authentic leader. However, another piece of the equation needs to be discussed. As I noted earlier, leaders have an opportunity to create moments of shared meaning through compassion, but they can take that a step further by practicing relatableness. It is when an authentic leader begins to relate with their colleagues in a way that is meaningful that the "authentic leader magic" really begins to take hold. This is the crux of the next chapter, in which we will explore the concept of relatableness.

(5)

RELATABLENESS

CREATING MICRO-MOMENTS
OF MEANING

Relatableness (n.)—The practice of an authentic leader who actively seeks out individuals to engage in meaningful, purposeful and compassionate conversations vertically and horizontally in an organization. A coined word derivative of relatable, from the root relate (v.).

DR. JAMES KELLEY

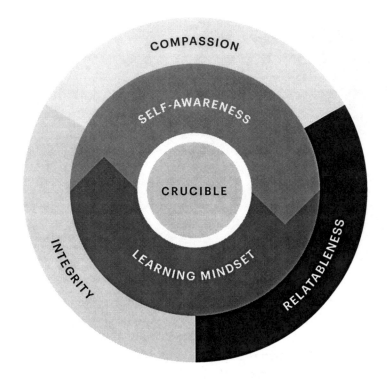

What Is Relatableness?

In the previous chapter, I stated that exercising compassion is an opportunity for an authentic leader to relate to those around them. Another aspect of relatableness is the use of charisma (for good, not evil). Using compassion or charisma provides authentic leaders with the opportunity to connect with individuals, both horizontally and vertically, in the organization and create micro-moments of meaning.

Relating to others may often remove leaders from their comfort zone. Many leaders believe that there is a demarcation in the leader-follower relationship, a line not to be crossed. A secondary cause of a lack of drive to relate to those around us is fear (it keeps popping up!)—fear of not being liked or fear of being judged—and these fears may be embedded in the culture of the organization. Let's first look at the role fear plays in impacting relatableness.

Think about a time when you and one other person, someone you know only casually, meet in the lunchroom or hallway. Awkward, right? As you recall that, you can hear yourself thinking, "Oh, man, do I have to talk? I just want to eat in quiet." Most of the time pleasantries are sufficient, such as "How are you?" or "Did you have a nice weekend?" You never really expect much of a response and hope to get out of the situation unscathed. But then, this one time, the other person actually gives you an answer beyond the single word "good," "great" or "okay," and the panic button has been pushed.

Then there's the time you decide to be bold and ask a follow-up question, like "Oh, it was good! Did you go to Bed Bath & Beyond? Home Depot?" and the other person stares at you uncomfortably and the look on their face is, "Why would you cross the professional-personal line, you nutjob?"

I've been there, and I am sure you have too—no better way to feel judged, rejected and sent back to your uncomfortable seventh-grade self. No one likes feeling judged or rejected, and the fear of those things is palpable.

Culture can also affect your ability to be relatable. In many workplace cultures, asking questions of someone you do not know is seen as rude. While writing this book, I sat in a coffee shop at the same seat for six hours a day, five days a week, for four and half weeks in Peníche, Portugal. I saw the same five staff people every day. They knew what I drank, what I ate, all the way down to the large beer at 4 p.m. to conclude my day of writing. But not once did any of the staff ask me my name, where I was from, what I was doing or if I was a CIA agent.

It amazed me. I befriended a local who also came in every day and I asked him about this. He told me that Portuguese people don't ask questions; they think it's rude. For the Portuguese culture, poking and prying is a no-no, and this is commonplace in other places I have lived, such as Japan and the United Arab Emirates.

A similar type of culture exists in the American workforce, where taking too deep an interest in someone's life is seen as crossing the professional-personal line. This relates back to the concept of the public/private self and trying to manage your image at work. I personally feel that professionalism has gotten in the way of being authentic. Just saying, if we cannot engage in a meaningful conversation because of the fear of being rejected or judged, it seems that we are missing the point of life.

While I was living in Perth, Australia, it always struck me that the line delineating one's professional and personal self was generally much blurrier, and it seemed that, overall, people enjoyed work—not necessarily *the* work, but being *at* work. I mean, where else on the planet do you have a "Sunday Session" to kick off the workweek? A Sunday Session is a meetup with your mates at the local pub, restaurant or hangout where you have some adult beverages and get home about 10 p.m—thus, the start of the workweek.

Regardless of the role of fear or culture, what I found through the interviews is that an authentic leader's first point of reference is to find a way to have purposeful and meaningful interactions by relating to people at all levels of the organization. Relating is the product of an authentic leader's curiosity, compassion, integrity and caring for those they lead.

But do employees really care about meaningful conversations? Daniel Pink, author of *Drive: The Surprising Truth about What Motivates Us*, believes the answer to be yes.[1] He found that humans have a deep-seated drive to relate to others and make meaningful connections, resulting in better engagement in the workplace. Pink uses self-determination theory (SDT) to explain this motivation. However, what is SDT? Let's take a look next.

Self-Determination Theory: Relatedness

SDT is the brainchild of Dr. Edward Deci and Dr. Richard Ryan,[2] who since 1980 have been engaged in a journey to understand the macro concepts that drive human motivation. SDT breaks down into three components: autonomy, competency and relatedness (this is different from relatableness, as we will discuss shortly). *Autonomy* is the process of empowerment. Your boss gives you the freedom to do your job, and you are accountable for success. *Competency* is achieved when an individual has the physical resources and relationships required to succeed at their job and can progress towards success. Finally, *relatedness* enters the picture when we feel that our efforts are recognized by others and that we are part of something beyond ourselves.

Relatedness is an outcome of relatableness. When you understand that people want to belong to something beyond themselves, you can help them create the circumstances and the environment to motivate them to act in ways above and beyond their normal to increase their engagement in the workplace. Many recent studies indicate that workplace engagement is between 20 percent and 30 percent. As pointed out in the introduction, Gallup's 2016 Employee Engagement survey, which spanned fifteen years, found that 31 percent of employees in U.S. and Canadian companies and a mere 13 percent of employees globally were engaged at work.[3] *Yikes!* That amounts to billions of dollars in lost productivity. So, understanding just the core motivation of individuals from the three standpoints—autonomy, competency and, specifically in this chapter, relatedness—allows you to understand that if you can relate to others and be relatable to them, then you can motivate them to do and be something greater.

One of my more popular interviews is with Dr. Richard Ryan, and when I asked him about the concept of motivation, he broke down the importance of relatedness. He shared the following intellectual nuggets:

DR. RICHARD RYAN: There's an area of relatedness, and here's one of the cheapest areas for intervention in corporations but one that's maybe the most neglected. So, in relatedness, you're really creating a sense that people do belong, that they're valued and significant in what they're doing, that they have something to contribute. I think we so often don't allow employees to understand and feel good about what they give to our companies. That's so much about what belongingness entails.

JAMES: That's funny, because that goes back to listening.

RICHARD: Absolutely, and then another thing that's very sacred to our interventions is supporting autonomy: allowing people to feel initiative, allowing them to feel like they have input and a voice, and they're not being pushed around by rewards and punishments only. All of these things have some little technical and nuanced aspects of it for managers, but they also have to do with how you structure a company. They're all things that you can intervene in. They're all things companies can change. They're all parts of [work] climates that, regardless of other bottom-line issues, these things can be moved, and that's why I really like interventions in this spirit, because it makes people happier, but it also makes companies more productive. (Episode 1)

In other words, authentic leaders who focus on relatableness will help create an emotional connection with their colleagues. It is in the process of being relatable that an authentic leader learns to read the environment and provide appropriate resources to create autonomy, promote competency and develop initiatives that are greater than oneself.

Creating Your Micro-Moments of Meaning

Academics and researchers Arlen Moller, Edward Deci and Andrew Elliott were curious as to what the value of relating is for a person who engages in repeated positive interactions.[4] What they found out—and I think this is really important—is that every day that an employee initiates a positive, relatable interaction with another person, the person who receives the positive interaction becomes incrementally more positive in that environment. Taking this result further, imagine the outcomes for all concerned when an authentic leader makes a deliberate effort to have a positive meaningful interaction with their colleagues. It doesn't have to be earth-shattering or take a large amount of time; it just has to be meaningful, genuine and positive.

If you play that out over every workday, over time you're going to create a positive work environment. And there's nothing better than that, because if you have a positive work environment, you have more loyal employees, higher levels of engagement, increased innovation and an all-around healthier financial bottom line. In addition, through incrementally positive interactions, an authentic leader can create a healthy emotional and physical work environment.

Let's envision a busy day at the office. Everyone arrives between 8:30 and 9:00—a generous start time, I am aware. You know that you have a series of deadlines that you have to meet. Now, imagine that your team leader, line manager, CEO or president comes storming through the office and doesn't make eye contact with anybody, doesn't stop to say hi, doesn't stop to ask how anyone's weekend was and has a threatening and intimidating physical posture. Net result? Demoralization. At the end of the day, it's almost as if you don't exist in the organization. You are merely an employee number that gets a paycheck every two weeks.

If you don't feel valued, if you don't feel like you're a part of something greater, then not only is your production going to lag, but your attitude won't be far behind. So when a team leader, manager or CEO takes the time to know who you are, to know your family, to know the name of your dog, you're going to work harder for them.

An authentic leader will ask his or her team, "Hey, how was your weekend?" "How did your wife do at the golf tournament?" The questions are genuine, not fluff. Though these may seem like trite questions, they go a long way in developing trust. To make the dialogue complete, when the staff ask the authentic leader the same types of questions, the leader is likely to share a story from *their* weekend. In this moment of sharing, a simple but meaningful bond is built. If such a bond exists already, it is reinforced. A leader is not required to know every detail about someone's life, but a leader will strive to find something in common to share.

One strategy I have is that when I do meet someone in their office (perhaps this will be a little creepy), I scan the office, looking for photos, the way the desks are organized, if there's a workout bag on the floor or some other item that helps me find common ground on which to share a story. Scanning the bookshelf can also be a great source of creating shared meaning.

How Can an Authentic Leader Use Relatableness across the Organization?

Individual to Individual

The first layer of this is the idea of individual-to-individual relatableness. This occurs in an everyday setting and is the most common interaction. This is a hallway or water-cooler conversation, but it serves as a way to interact with your colleagues in a personable way. This is also where relatableness and compassion intersect. When we show compassion to our colleagues, opportunities are created for sharing similar compassionate experiences.

There is a commencement speech that was given at the University of Western Australia in 2013 by the actor Tim Minchin.[5] It's a great speech, and I recommend you have a listen to it on YouTube. Minchin rattles off a number of attributes or characteristics he believes constitute the character of a good person. One such "good person test" is how a potential business partner treats a restaurant's waitstaff. For Tim, treating those with the least amount of power with sincere respect provides evidence of the potential partner's kindness and character. Moving this concept to the office, how do your executives treat those with the least amount of power? Leaders or co-workers who hold values and beliefs that everyone is a valued member of the team will also go out of their way to create shared micro-moments of meaning.

Dr. Joel Bennett and his company Organizational Wellness & Learning Systems work with organizations around a number of health and wellness objectives. In our conversation, Dr. Bennett and I were discussing the importance of relationships when he said the following:

How can I be present and show up to you, James? How can this conversation flow? Then what are the synchronicities that can occur while we're talking? What are the coincidences that occur? Yesterday we talked about your wife. There was a real synchronicity there for me. When I'm in that space, then I'm operating at a level of, really, true connecting. It's not a transaction anymore. For me, it's being able to show up in the moment with others and *be* that, *with* that. When I'm operating that way, when I'm coming to a relationship that way, strategy completely goes away because I'm just a vulnerable person interacting with another vulnerable person. That's where the transformation happens. (Episode 13)

As I mentioned, and will probably mention again, if you spend over eight hours a day at work, wouldn't you want to be yourself as much as possible? Wouldn't you want to care about the people you work with? Workplaces still suffer from retroactive cultures that we've been holding on to since the sixties and seventies, in which a demilitarized zone is created between emotions and rationality. I'm not saying that it is okay to let irrational emotions be expressed in the workplace, but I believe healthy emotions do have a place.

Going back to this idea of integrity, compassion and self-awareness, the idea of relatableness is this: "I'm aware enough to know my strengths and weakness, and I'm confident enough and have enough integrity that I can share this with the people around me to know that they're not going to judge me." Chances are, if you're in a leader-follower environment in which the leader is being transparent and authentic and relating to people and the follower believes in outdated paradigms, the follower will self-select out of that workplace. The organization is no worse off for losing those who think they cannot thrive in a relatable environment.

I recently interviewed a CEO who made it very clear that she does not practice relatableness in her organization. Everything is business and nothing is personal. No "How was your weekend?"

"How is your family?" or "Are you doing okay?" It wasn't that she doesn't care, but she just felt it was unnecessary. When I pushed her on the impact of the leader-follower relationship, she indicated that she believed it was good. I have no reason to believe that the relationships there are not trusting and meaningful; rather, they are just not personal. But it got me thinking, "What would happen if there were opportunities to create shared meaning?"

Creating Shared Organizational Micro-Moment Experiences

The authentic leader realizes that creating shared experiences, no matter how big or, more likely, small, will have a lasting impact on organizational culture. This moves beyond the individual-to-individual connection to focus on creating a culture of authentic interactions that break down actual or perceived barriers to the team's success.

Going back to the work of Deci and Ryan, individuals in an organization are internally motivated to be a part of something greater than themselves. To make that possible, organizational leaders need to create the environment and opportunities of micro shared moments. Micro shared moments are the moments in an organization that seem meaningless and inconsequential to the overall culture. However, it is in these moments that individuals in the organization begin to buy into the culture of relatableness.

Take, for example, the simple pleasantries that occur while walking through the hall. To create a micro-moment can be as simple as stopping, looking the other person in the eye and asking them how they're doing. It isn't so much about the question, as we all typically engage in basic pleasantries: the key is the body language used. Acts like this can have the greatest impact in creating shared meaning experiences. Though this example comes back to the individual-to-individual level, it goes deeper, because the culture of micro-moments develops with authentic leaders who understand the power of relatableness.

Finally, as noted previously, Arlen Moller, Edward Deci and Andrew Elliott conducted a study that found that the more moments of happiness, kindness and general relatableness that are created, the higher the buildup of goodwill in the organization. Thus, both micro-moments at the one to one and team levels are essential for creating a culture of relatableness. However, this culture only occurs when leaders and followers show up to work as their authentic self.

The Fallacy of Charm

Dr. Michael Maccoby, president of The Maccoby Group in Washington, D.C., is a frequent *Harvard Business Review* contributor and often writes on narcissism and leadership. In an *HBR* article published in 2000, Maccoby describes what I call the "fallacy of charm" effect. The fallacy of charm effect occurs when a person leads by false pretenses and uses their natural charisma to manipulate those around them to achieve a goal that results in a less desirable outcome. Here is how Maccoby describes these leaders:

Despite the warm feelings that charisma can evoke, narcissists are typically not comfortable with their own emotions. They listen only for the kind of information they seek. They don't learn easily from others. They don't like to teach but prefer to indoctrinate and make speeches. They dominate meetings with subordinates. The result for the organization is greater internal competitiveness at a time when everyone is already under as much pressure as they can possibly stand. Perhaps the main problem is that the narcissist's faults tend to become even more pronounced as he becomes more successful.[6]

Maccoby lists several overarching attributes of a leader who uses charisma and narcissism for evil. As you read through the following list, see if you can think of someone who has some of these attributes:

- is sensitive to criticism
- is a poor listener
- is lacking in empathy
- has a distaste for mentoring
- has an intense desire to compete
- is more interested in controlling others than through the use of discipline itself

These characteristics suggest that some "leaders" are less interested in people and more interested in themselves and in potentially manipulating an environment.

Let me create a picture of what it may look like if a leader or colleague who is low in relatableness defaults to exhibiting aspects of the fallacy of charm effect. Think back to see if a colleague comes to mind who can't wait to talk, cuts you off in midsentence or seems to always have a story that's just one notch better than yours. I call this person the "one-upper." You know the type: they aren't listening to a damn thing you are saying. They're waiting for you to take a breath so that they can jump in. Essentially, they're waiting to talk, not listening with intent.

Taking a leadership perspective, there are leaders who share with you a lifestyle you cannot relate to, almost making you feel bad because you don't belong to a particular socioeconomic class or lifestyle. This could be a leader who brags about flying around on private jets, driving a fancy car, and wearing expensive clothes or accessories. I don't fault those who have done well for themselves—this is more about leaders who believe flaunting wealth will motivate their employees and who disregard others' current needs. It can create resentment, and it demonstrates a leader's lack of relatableness with those whose circumstances are less privileged and who might prefer to support charities over aspiring to privilege. For those leaders who feel the need to show off their wealth, it may be about misplaced motivation or a lack of confidence, or it may be the product of the culture of the work environment (which suggests it needs an authentic leader fix).

Some leaders who are low in relatableness have situational relatableness issues. Have you been in environments where you walk into a meeting, everyone sits down to start and several people instantly whip out their phones and start typing? They are not present, not trying to connect with their colleagues in the room on a professional level. The perception they create is that they're super busy, super important and super not interested in being at the meeting. This behavior is rude and sends a negative signal to colleagues who *are* present that their time is not important. The team leader needs to call out such behavior, recognizing that we're all busy but that we need to show respect and all deserve respect.

Finally, there are leaders who embrace many aspects of the fallacy of charm effect, rise to the top of an organization and use manipulation, intimidation and indoctrination to get their employees to do what they want. If you work for a leader who is like this, run! If you are a leader like this, ask yourself, "How do I want to be remembered when I am dead?" If you are a leader who exudes many aspects of the above list, you will probably answer by exclaiming your greatness.

The Art of Oversharing

As I wrote this chapter, I found myself asking, and you perhaps are thinking this now, "Where is the TMI (too much information) line drawn in an organizational setting?" This is an important question, and it concerns individual tolerance. It's difficult to draw a line in the sand and say that X is too far but Y is okay. Many variables may impact that line, including an organization's attitude towards, among other things, creating a culture in which information is shared openly; supporting individual belief systems and individual self-confidence; making it safe for employees to trust one another; and enabling the alignment of the public versus private self. For organizations that believe in creating shared personal and private experiences, it all starts with trusting those around you.

This raises the question of what counts as too much personal information. I don't think an environment of drama is healthy, but I do believe that if a colleague is going through a tough time, such as a death in the family, a divorce, the illness of a child or some other traumatic event, sharing their feelings with a trusting authentic leader is a must. It not only allows the colleague who is having a hard time to keep their manager abreast of their situation, but it also provides a chance for the leader to create a moment of compassion through a shared experience.

Finally, when it comes to your colleagues sharing personal information with you, it is up to you to become involved or not. If the problem is beyond your personal or professional ability, practice your integrity. Let the other person know that you are uncomfortable with them sharing particular personal information. You never know—you may be the first person to tell them that they are falling into TMI.

Three Leaders on How Authentic Leaders Relate

For this section of the book, I selected three leaders who came from super-humble beginnings: not a lot of money, not a lot of wealth and not a lot of opportunity. They all started working when they were really young (as did *many* of the leaders). Before I introduce these leaders, let me set the stage.

As I noted in the introduction, the concepts for this book only started to jell after I had completed about fifty interviews. The idea of relatableness was not something I set out to explore, but what I found is that for some leaders, especially those discussed in this section, a cocktail of experiences led them to espouse the ideals of relatableness. The authentic leaders below illustrate some of what can go into that cocktail.

Jeffrey Hayzlett and Connie Pheiff came from lower-income families and, some would argue, a difficult social environment. Sean Geehan was the sixth out of seven children in his family and was given a lot of latitude to explore and develop. Like Jeffrey and Connie, Sean was not raised in a wealthy family and earned the money he needed to spend on himself. And they all surpassed expectations they had set for themselves, as well as those set for them by others, and all reached very high levels of professional success.

It seemed to me, based on what was revealed during my interviews with them and across many other interviews I conducted, that the crucible playing a significant role in this process concerns survival. In surviving, especially during their childhood, these leaders figured out how to maneuver in an environment where there are life risks. One coping mechanism for survival for many people begins with the question, "How do I relate to the people around me?" Survival also taught them to be much more self-aware and to read a situation to figure out what sets of actions, both verbal and physical, are going to best pan out so that they can succeed in the moment.

Connie Pheiff: From a Rebel to, Well, a *Nice* Rebel (Episode 98)

Connie Pheiff is a former CEO of Girl Scouts and currently an entrepreneur and podcast host. She was raised in an environment where she essentially took care of her cousins and a woman she called "Grandma," beginning when she was only about 10 years old. She faced adversity and negativism. Connie shares her perspective:

I remember back to the age of 8, 9, 10 years old. My role in the family was taking care of all my cousins that would come [over] every day, so the house was cleaned every morning. I would make everybody's breakfast, I would make everybody's lunch, including lunch for their parents. I would walk the kids to school—like, *all* my cousins to school. That's when they would have their kindergarten. I would have to come back home at lunchtime, swallow my food, make sure everybody was fed, go back to school for the afternoon, take other cousins back for the afternoon classes and then come home and make dinner, clean the house.

Later on in the interview, Connie spoke about the woman she took care of. At the time, her mother was adamant that she needed to quit school at 16 and start working full-time.

So living there, education wasn't important. I was being told when I would turn 16, I was going to quit school. The carrot was instead of riding my bicycle, [the woman] was going to let me get a car that I would pay for myself. Then I could quit school and go to work at the sewing factory down the street.

I cried. I mean, I prayed. I did everything I could to say, "Please, dear God, I don't want to quit school." Although my grades sucked, I didn't put any effort into it, but school was still . . . It started getting more important to me. Well, it turned out—and this sounds horrible—she died a month before my sixteenth birthday, and I never cried. I call it a gift. After she died, then through the rest of high school, I did live with my parents for a bit of time, but that didn't work out very well.

I am sure you are questioning my sanity in providing Connie as an example of relatableness, but let me tie this story together.

JAMES: It would seem to me that, when you talk about the idea of emotional connection, emotional engagement, it almost all predicates back to when you're a child and wanting to connect with people, and when you had the ability to do it and control that infrastructure of connection—you thrive on that as an adult.

CONNIE PHEIFF: Yeah.

JAMES: And to do that—to me, at least—that's one of the tenets that I have, and it's something that I'm writing about: being an authentic leader. It is being able to relate to people. One of the best ways you relate, and I think that's kind of one of the shticks of my podcasts, is that I share stories about my life too, and how vulnerable I've been. And when you do that, there's a trust that's automatically built with the people around you, because you're a human being as well.

CONNIE: Right. It's that authenticity, and that is what I talk about in leadership because so often we get into leadership positions—and I know I'm guilty of it . . . If I had to walk into a country club, I was like, "I don't belong here." It's that imposter syndrome as well that we have that I . . . If people only knew who I really am and what I really did. Why would they respect me? But when you allow that authenticity . . . I mean, you don't have to spill your guts and say . . .

JAMES: Sure, yeah. There's a line, though.

CONNIE: Right, there is a line, but when you allow that authenticity to come across, that's when people are able to relate to you. When

I finally accepted that for myself and shared that big lie that I was holding all of those years, and then again, five years ago, finding out the truth about my family and why things happened the way they did, the guilt... Although I worked on it all these years, I still had a strong hold on that guilt, and when I found out, five years ago, when I let that go, it was like my... Again, a pivotal point in my life where everything changed. I like people now.

JAMES: Good for you. You're a recovering people-hater, so I appreciate that.

Connie's revelation that life throws you curve balls and that you have choices as to how you react to them was an important outcome for her. It allowed her to realize that all the misfortune that occurred when she was a child only provided her experience as an adult to tackle life's hard realities. People will either like you for who you are or they will not. Connie's path to authenticity, like so many others', was not linear. But through a developed self-awareness and four decades, Connie learned that being yourself is much easier for her and also more relatable for others.

Jeffrey Hayzlett: You Can Take the Guy Out of South Dakota, but You Can't Take South Dakota Out of the Guy (Episode 95)

We met Jeffrey Hayzlett earlier in the book. His parents divorced when he was in his teens and he moved with his dad to South Dakota. Jeffrey was a child in a military family that moved every three to four years, so he had to reestablish and reposition himself in the school hierarchy, and in that hierarchy, reassert his will. When he moved to South Dakota, he fell in love with the state. Jeffrey describes his experience as spiritual, and as the best time of his life—so much so that even with a majority of his business on the coasts, he still makes South Dakota his home with his wife and family. As you speak to Jeffrey, he comes across as the guy you would stand with at the bar to have a shot of whiskey and shoot the breeze. It was clear that moving to South Dakota and having to work at a young age had a big impact on Jeffrey, and within the crucible that impacted his relatableness was his meager upbringing:

Think about it. Look, I'm a poor kid. Some would even maybe call it white trash to some extent, or trailer park trash or whatever you might think. I've actually had people say that to me, which I'm proud of. But my point is, there's a lot of people, a lot more money, a lot more things, a lot more opportunity, and I used to think that you needed those things—and you don't. And so it took me a long time to realize that, no, I'm just as good as these guys are. I'm just as smart as these guys are. In fact, I'm smarter. I'm brighter, I'm quicker, I'm faster.

This helps put Jeffrey's background into perspective, but there's another thing that I believe was critical for Jeffrey's ability to use relatableness for a positive outcome. I prodded him about the role that being a military child had on his ability to adapt to new situations.

But, yeah, I do think every person that I went to school with—and by the way, I used to see those people at various schools at different air force bases around the world—so yeah, those people . . . I tend to think that we're a little . . . I don't want to say we're more well rounded, but we certainly have a lot more exposure to the more worldly things or things in life that make us just get over it. To get to another point, I'm sure that maybe when you first met your wife, you said, "Well, geez, that was kind of weird. That's not healthy that you've lived in all these places." People say that to me all the time. "Well, that's sort of weird."

Well, no. Weird is going to the same school, living in the same city all your fricking life, knowing the same . . .

The point I was trying to make with Jeffrey and that I've witnessed with Mary (a military brat) is that because Jeffrey was forced to adapt, relate and make friends every three to four years, he learned how to be relatable on *others'* terms—meaning that he would look for shared experiences when he met someone new and bond over those shared experiences to create a social network in a hurry.

Sean Geehan: One Mango and One Connection at a Time (Episode 78)

Sean Geehan is the CEO of Geehan Group, an organization that specializes in working with Fortune 1000 companies to create and manage customer advisory boards and provide strategic planning services. In addition, Sean has launched a new project called Slate Homes, where he and his team are building sustainable, smart housing communities. He honed his relatableness skills by selling mangoes in Hawaii at the age of 10. As the sixth of seven kids, Sean was left to his own devices at an early age. Plus, he learned that if he wanted money from his parents, they didn't have any: he needed to go earn it. Hence, selling mangoes. But what selling mangoes really taught Sean was the power of connecting with others—seeing how relatableness leads to success.

Sean graduated from selling mangoes to buying and selling companies. During our conversation, I asked him how he views his impact on corporate culture:

JAMES: Do you think that creating that organizational culture is reflective of who you are, or is it reflective of the different pieces of the puzzle?

SEAN GEEHAN: I think it's reflective of who I am. Inherently, I trust people. And that's why I'm not going to sit there and look for the one person, the one action, that somebody takes that's taking advantage of me. Life's too short. Over time, you'll come to know who those people are, and they'll vet themselves out.

I think in consulting companies, it's very hard to hide ... You've got to be a producer, you've got to do something, right? I just let that go. There are so many people that I meet with who are CEOS of companies that are smaller. They're like, "My employees are like this. I've got to stay on top of them." I'm like, "Why?"

Either you're bringing the wrong people in or you're just not giving them the latitude—just let them go. Yeah, there's going to be somebody that takes off or that doesn't do the right thing, or makes a bad decision, or is lazy, whatever it is. You can't sit there and start to look for that. Look for the good, and try to amplify it and reward it, and I think you'll start to attract better people. I feel like we've done that. We've got great people here, and I love where we are today and the position we're in to move forward.

I have known Sean for twenty-plus years and can recall a hundred stories of how he's walked into a room and made an instant connection with the person who has the least power in the relationship. Sean takes this and applies it to his own corporation. In our discussion above, Sean indirectly states that by engaging in a conversation with his colleagues, he can gain a better understanding of each of their strengths and weaknesses so that he can help them better use their natural gifts in their organizations.

What Do These Stories Have in Common?

One theme that stands out from my interviews with Connie, Jeffrey and Sean, as well as other leaders, is the ability to relate to other individuals no matter the point those individuals have reached in their personal journeys. Most leaders have developed this ability over time through personal crucibles, such as a military upbringing or childhood challenges in general. Regardless of how each leader developed their relatableness, these three shared their ability to embrace where they came from, what situations inform their being and the ability to use those circumstances to be self-confident, compassionate, curious and transparent.

During the interviews, I found myself often imagining having a beer, grabbing dinner or taking a walk with these leaders to talk about their core personal philosophy. Finally, I think it's important here that Connie, Jeffrey and Sean didn't come from wealth—they earned it. I don't fault anyone who came from wealth, but these three and many others started working early with a cross-section of society. From this they learned that individuals are made up of different stripes and colors. It is these stripes and colors that these leaders used to navigate their rise in the corporate world and use now to build stronger, more meaningful relationships.

How Do I Use Relatableness?

When I was working on my MBA, I briefly lived with a guy named Joe. Joe is exceptionally talented at talking with people in a way that makes them feel special. It is a true gift he has, and one he uses for good rather than evil. I was always impressed with how he would put a smile on someone's face and create a single moment that left the person with a memory of that interaction. Though Joe is seven or eight years younger, I learned a lot from watching him interact. I took mental notes of what he said, how he said it, even when he said it. The reason I share this story is that even at 23, Joe had a skill that many would desire to have in their arsenal. Joe was a natural at being relatable.

I always thought I was someone who was good at being relatable, but I realized that I don't move the masses. As time has passed, I have continued to develop relatableness as a skill, using the *Executives After Hours* podcast as a vehicle to practice and enhance the art. During the podcast I tell stories to create shared experiences so that I can build trust with the guest. Even as I develop my skills around being relatable, I can see some similarities between how Connie, Jeffrey and Sean and I grew up. After being raised in a lower-middle-class environment with limited educational resources to work with, I slowly worked my way up. I didn't complete my PhD until I was 36, but what I did do was acquire a multitude of experiences, some of which were way out of my comfort zone; meet individuals from around the world; and develop a bank of experiences that I can draw on in any number of instances.

I mentioned earlier that when meeting an individual face to face I look around the office or room to find something we have in common. I always want to find a common starting position for our conversation. I think part of this drive can be connected to my being the youngest by five years and having often been left to my own devices for entertainment. Additionally, there was a surrogate family I spent many summers around during my childhood. This family was mixed race (Anglo and Hispanic), hippies, and had a huge cross-section of friends from Native American and Hispanic, poor and wealthy backgrounds. Just spending time at their house taught me that we, as humans, have more in common than we do differences and that the goal should always be to focus on the similarities.

Final Thoughts (for Now) on Relatableness

Relatableness, as I see it, is a trait that for some comes easy, whereas others find it a challenge. I believe that relatableness can be developed and cultivated, opening up more opportunities to create meaningful connections. The importance of this skill cannot be understated in the development of trust for the leader-follower relationship, but it has to start from a place of genuine interest and curiosity.

Historically, organizations have shied away from encouraging meaningful sharing. However, Mark Crowley, who we met in chapter 2, believes that organizations that promote this cultural stance are full of crap. Here is what Mark says about making meaningful connections with colleagues:

The taboo is that we think that's messy, we don't want to get caught up in all that. The minute you start to get personal with people, [you think] that they're going to take advantage of that and you're not going to be able to make tough decisions. That's all just complete crap. People feel heard. They feel that they've been given a voice. They feel they have a trusting relationship with their boss, so they feel safe. They don't feel like, "I wonder if my boss thinks that I'm doing a good job." That's a really disempowering kind of a thought process. You can take people out of that by saying, "No, I picked you. I'm happy you're on my team. I love the work that you're doing. I want to help you grow better." Everybody's got a different dream. Some people want to proceed and become CEO, some people just want to keep doing what they're doing, but they still want to learn. (Episode 45)

These are pretty powerful words, and ones that I agree with. A leader who genuinely understands the power of the personal connection has the ability to shape the culture in the organization. When personal connections are exponentially multiplied across the organization, the potential for magic can occur. However, the magic only occurs when a leader embraces relatableness as a personal attribute for creating intimate encounters. Thus, it should be a mission for an organization to create and cultivate an environment for micro-moments of meaning. The result is the deepening and strengthening of respect and loyalty across the organization. Leaders are the catalyst.

Let's Work on Being More Relatable

Turning to my colleagues Seth and Kara, let's look at some things you can do to work on being more open, approachable and relatable.

1. *Do Dale—Dale Carnegie training.* Dale Carnegie is the well-known author of the iconic book *How to Win Friends and Influence People*, originally published in 1936.[7] His book is still widely read and has been updated to account for the world of the internet. Its premise is that we can create success—professional and personal—through relationships. Born out of this book was the Dale Carnegie Institute, where individuals can be trained in how to apply the concepts. Members of Mary's family completed this course and were amazed by the program. They found that the course provided them with tools to better maneuver various environments while making those they engage with feel better about the interaction.

2. *Interest begets interest.* This is as true in business as it is in dating. Ask curiosity questions ("Help me understand how you came to that conclusion?" "What makes you interested in that pursuit?"). Asking curiosity questions is an excellent way

to gather information about others, and information about others can be a powerful tool in leadership

3. *Just care.* Respond to what the other person says as if you care about what they said rather than as an opportunity to share something similar that happened to you. Probe deeper. Show your interest.

4. *Use the mirror effect.* While speaking with another person, focus entirely on them. Notice what they're doing with their hands, how their eyes are moving and the inflection of their voice. Be *with* the person in front of you (mindful listening).

5. *Watch your leadership posture.* Practice an open posture (for example, arms uncrossed). Using an open posture gives the unconscious message that you are kind, trusting and open for a meaningful conversation.

6. *Put it down and walk away.* Minimize the use of technology when with someone else. Avoid whipping out your phone to look something up, and the like. As mentioned earlier, some people in a meeting are there only physically, not mentally or emotionally. And let's be honest, that's just plain rude. Give respect and be present.

Where Do We Go from Here?

So far in this journey, we have discussed a number of factors that lead to authentic leadership: a crucible creates the opportunity for a leader to change their self-awareness. From the change in self-awareness, an authentic leader will experience a change in integrity and compassion. In this chapter, we discussed the role of relatableness as a new variable in the authentic leader equation. As a result, our equation is transformed again, with the addition of relatableness (R).

Crucible = $(\Delta SA) + (\Delta I + \Delta C + \Delta R)$ = Authentic Leadership

There is one final piece of the equation critical to the authentic leader's development, and that is the role that learning has on their ability to be curious about their own personal growth, their growth in their profession and the growth of their colleagues. Thus, the final input into the equation of the Authentic Leadership Model is learning from the crucible, learning from the environment, and learning throughout a journey to authenticity. Next up, let's explore a leader's curiosity to learn.

(6)

LEARNING
BE CURIOUS LIKE A CHILD

I think you always seem like you're in a hurry trying to get somewhere. I think at 25 you think you know everything, so I would say, listen more. You don't really have the answer key, genius. You have plenty to learn. As a matter of fact, if you're lucky you'll be learning your whole life . . . Listen more, write more and talk less.

RICHARD BOLTE, CEO of BDP International,
a global logistics company (Episode 87)

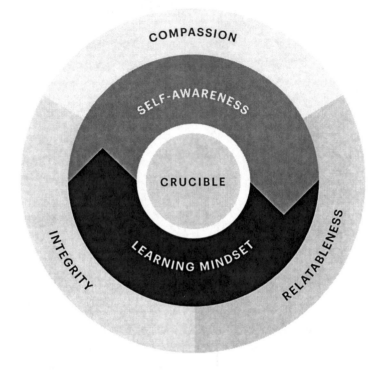

To Learn for the Sake of Learning

Professional and personal growth comes only from learning, and leaders often discuss and share stories of their learning from failures and successes. Many of the guests on the podcast discussed their joy in learning. Learning came for them in many forms—from feedback, colleagues, personal relationships, successes and failures, research and study, and everything in between. Authentic leaders were informed and inspired by their ability to apply what they learned to their professional and personal growth.

Andrew Schirmer, president of McCann Global Health, was the third interview on the podcast. He responded to my curiosity about where he focused on learning to develop his leadership skills:

I think another kind of takeaway is influence, positive and negative, that can come from anywhere. Try to know the difference but don't be closed-minded, because we can learn lessons by stepping out of ourselves every day, and I've learned as much having worked in the ad-comms [advertising communications] business. I learned as much from the non-health clients and discussions they're having around problems as I do from my colleagues within health. (Episode 3)

Andrew surveys the landscape to gain vital insights for the business, and uses them to gain an advantage in the marketplace.

Dr. Richard Ryan, founding father of self-determination theory, said to me, "Intrinsic motivation is just an example of the proactive nature of people. People like to learn. They find pleasure in learning" (episode 1). So if, intrinsically, people enjoy learning, why do some hug the tree of learning while others treat learning like it's bad tofu? Let's turn to Carol Dweck.

Growth versus Fixed Mindset: Which Do You Have?

Dr. Carol Dweck, in her 2006 book *Mindset*,[1] set out to uncover why some people grow intellectually and professionally while others are okay with the status quo. She found that it wasn't because those who were satisfied with the status quo thought they were awesome—well, kind of. Dweck developed the concept of growth mindset and fixed mindset. *Growth mindset* occurs when a person is learning oriented, desires mastery, devours feedback and seeks encouragement for effort. A person with a *fixed mindset*, on the other hand, is concerned with performance goals, wants favorable judgments from others and prefers the status quo. Dweck explains that a person's mindset is not entirely on the growth side or fixed, but rather on a continuum, based on the context and situation.

For example, someone may desire to be an elite triathlete and so will spend a lot of time learning about the nuances of the sport, will welcome feedback and will continually assess their performance. For all things related to their athletic prowess, that person is growth focused. However, in a workplace setting, they may feel as they have the right (and unassailable) job-specific skills and so will get defensive when colleagues provide feedback, or will measure their work performance against the achievements of their colleagues and fret about their legacy.

So how do you know which side you fall on? Dweck spent twenty-plus years investigating growth and fixed mindset and has come up with a series of questions to ask yourself. Take a minute and reflect on a recent challenge that you faced and the reaction you had during the challenge, and answer the following:

- Did you feel overly anxious? Did a voice in your head put up roadblocks that prevented you from conquering the challenge?
- When you faced a setback in your career, did you feel incompetent or defeated? Did you look for an excuse for the failure?
- What was your response the last time you received feedback at work or home? Did you become defensive, angry or feel defeated, instead of interested in learning from the feedback?
- What happens when you see a colleague who's better than you excelling at a task you value? Do you feel envious and threatened, or do you feel eager to learn?

If your responses skewed to looking to appoint blame or find excuses rather than look for an opportunity to learn, then you are likely stuck in a fixed mindset.

Think about the leaders in your organization or other leaders you have met or even reported to. Those with a fixed mindset will claim successes even though they were part of a team effort. They go out of their way to make sure that those around them know who produced the solution. They tend to have big egos and believe they are better than many of their peers, and aren't shy about saying so to their direct reports. Many leaders who have a fixed mindset mask their insecurities with boastfulness, place blame on others for the failure and stifle their critics. If the fixed mindset leader is at a senior level in the organization, they can be abusive and controlling, and this ends up permeating the whole organization. The result is a fixed mindset company that will struggle to adapt and grow.

Take the 2001 Enron debacle. There were many case studies done on what went wrong at Enron. One key finding was that the leadership was focused more on protecting their personal investments than looking out for the shareholders. Further, Jeffrey Skilling, the CEO, often placed blame on others, lashed out at the media and lacked compassion for those his actions harmed. Skilling is currently hanging out in a concrete house serving out a twenty-four-year jail sentence. Enron is a prime example of an organization that was infested with leadership that lacked authenticity and acted with a fixed mindset.[2] Then there was WorldCom. In 2002, WorldCom was caught committing a $3.8 billion accounting fraud. CEO Bernie Ebbers had a clear strategy of growth by acquisition but struggled to show consistent returns for his shareholders. Feeling the pressure and lacking integrity, Ebbers cooked the books and is now spending twenty-five years behind bars.

Enron's and WorldCom's leadership actions wiped out their employees' retirement funds. There are many more examples like Enron and WorldCom, and across these, many of the causes of failure reside with leadership. According to Dweck, leaders similar to Skilling and Ebbers typically shut down feedback from those around them and instead seek to create a cultures of "yes."[3] As a result, they never receive critical feedback to use to weigh and balance their decisions. Result: a fixed mindset.

Leaders with a growth mindset believe that learning and experiences can impact a person's behavior by fostering development. Leaders with a growth mindset want to own their failures. If the failures are their responsibility, they put them on display for others to learn from. They use these moments to create micro-growth mindset moments. These leaders never claim others' successes, and they spend time listening to, crediting and nurturing their colleagues. Finally, leaders that have a growth mindset provide honest feedback, believe that teams create success, and believe in their own and their team's professional and personal development.[4]

Jack Welch was CEO of General Electric from 1981 to 2001 and grew the company value by 4,000 percent during that time. Known to be direct and hard charging, Welch is seen by many experts as one of the best business leaders ever. Bill George, former CEO of Medtronic, took the company's market capitalization from $1.1 billion to $60 billion, averaging an annual 35 percent increase. Finally, you can argue the likes of Mark Zuckerberg, CEO of Facebook, Meg Whitman, former president and CEO of Hewlett Packard Enterprise, and Oprah Winfrey (not sure she requires an introduction) all possess a growth mindset. Welch, George, Zuckerberg, Whitman and Winfrey, through their time at the helm (past and present), grew their organizations by keeping their ear to the ground, listening to others, giving credit and nurturing their internal and external stakeholders, leading to financial success for their organizations.

Learning Is the Power behind Authentic Leadership

Learning is the power authentic leaders use to strengthen their identity and grow as a leader. Let's review how we have arrived at this juncture, where the leader recognizes that an authentic self is emerging and that supporting and growing it is essential.

In chapter 1 we broke down the role of crucibles and the three different layers. *Bizarro* is the first and most basic level of a crucible. Bizzaro crucibles occur when individuals are placed in a unique new environment; for example, when moving to a distant and unfamiliar location or starting a new job. *Forced break* is the second layer and is marked by life making choices for you. You could call this a life nudge. This may be getting laid off, going back to school or deciding to go on a spiritual journey. *Avalanche* is the final layer, and is the crucible that feels like the world is coming down around you and you find it metaphorically hard to breathe. These crucibles might be the death of a loved one, a divorce or a bankruptcy. However, each person's crucible is unique, and no one can qualify or quantify a crucible for someone else. That said, generally speaking, the more significant the crucible, the more opportunities to work on self-awareness. Thus, crucibles create opportunities for growth.

In chapter 2 we discussed self-awareness, shedding light on the impact it can have on a leader's success. This is not to say that success requires self-awareness: there are plenty of successful leaders who are financially successful but are far from authentic. But authentic leaders who embrace self-awareness as a tool for growth look inward for personal improvement, which results in better leadership. I believe that leaders who are highly self-aware strengthen personal and professional integrity and compassion, and take opportunities to create shared meaning with their colleagues. This process is ongoing—an authentic leader loves to learn.

Overall, a leader's crucible is an opportunity to learn, and that learning can permeate their growth of integrity, compassion and relatableness. Without the desire to grow, evolve and strengthen their leadership skills, a person is like a boulder—big and hard, and you get nothing out of it when you try to move it. Additionally, though the premise of this chapter is that learning leads to growth, it may be even more important for a leader to learn theories and topics that are not in line with their current thinking. It is easy to prove a current point of view, one that you're known for, but carrying around accepted thinking for too long makes you stale. As with receiving feedback from your colleagues, it's important to read varying opinions around your industry to flip your expertise on its head and test your assumptions.

Three Authentic Leaders Who Exhibit a Growth Mindset

As has been the case in every chapter, it is hard to select the most valuable examples from the interviews, but I did my best to provide three leaders that I believe exemplify learning and the growth mindset. Joe Friel, Tommy Katzenellenbogen and Joe De Sena each used a crucible and moment to reflect on who they are, where they're going and the learning that has to occur to move their journey along. Further, if you listen to their complete interviews, you'll find that they are constantly taking their beliefs and opinions and hitting them with a cricket bat (for my Commonwealth friends).

Joe Friel: Legendary Triathlon Coach, Innovator and Really Nice Guy (Episode 59)

I had the pleasure of interviewing Joe Friel. If you have ever wanted to learn the ins and outs of triathlon training, Joe Friel's *The Triathlete's Training Bible* is the go-to book. Joe has carved a life out of expanding his mindset around triathlon and endurance sports in general, and is the best example I've seen of a growth mindset. At just over 70 and with over forty years of coaching, research and writing experience around triathlon, Joe could easily hang up his writing chops. But every time Joe answers one question about endurance sports, another pops up. Below is a conversation about a recent book Joe wrote and why he continues to write:

Well, I wrote a book back in about 1997 or so called *Cycling Past 50* because I had just turned 50 and I wanted to see if I can help people learn about training for aging athletes. So I wrote it, but the basis of the book, as I always do, is to do the research—you know, exercise science sort of stuff. And there wasn't much science out there back in the late nineties. But the little bit I found indicated that when you got to about 70 there was a rapid drop in performance for athletes. It was rather steady until that point, and then all of the sudden performance dropped off real rapidly.

So, fast-forward now to 2013; I'm six months out from my 70th birthday and I'm contemplating what I had written about back in the late nineties—about how when you get to age 70 performance drops off rather rapidly, and that kind of concerned me.

And so I began to think about it. The more I thought about it, the more I realized I had to go back and read that research.

So in June of 2015 I gave myself my birthday present—that was about six months before my birthday in December. So I decided I would go back and just read all of the research I could find on the subject, and so I started reading it. And I read it every day for six months, basically. I'm sure I missed a day or two along the way someplace. But I was poring over these studies to see what I could learn . . . I would post a blog on what I was learning about aging athletes and I began to get lots of emails and responses on my blog from older athletes saying that they were learning a lot.

By the time I was like four months into this project, I realized that these people were really hungry for this information ... And so consequently, I contacted a publisher and said, "Hey, I'd like to write a book on this subject," and they said actually, yeah, they'd been thinking about a book like that themselves. And so that's how it got started—from my own aging process.

Joe is a great example of a lifelong learner who consistently seeks to gain a better understanding about his body and endurance sports. But on top of this, Joe goes back to "I bet others would benefit from X." Joe's learning is based on self-awareness and compassion for others. It's a pretty powerful place to lead from.

Tommy Katzenellenbogen, Chief Strategy Officer at Cron Systems (Episode 85)

Besides having the longest last name in history, Tommy spent fourteen years in the Israeli air force—learning. Learning about himself, about processes and about how to be a leader. Tommy went on to earn his MBA from Cambridge Judge Business School, at the University of Cambridge in the U.K. Without an undergraduate degree, Tommy talked his way into Cambridge and convinced the admissions team that his fourteen years of air force leadership (Israeli Defense Force, infantry officer's training, and Israeli Air Force) and the academic equivalent of undergraduate classes were enough for admission. His persistence paid off. I asked Tommy how those fourteen years in military service shaped his view of learning:

TOMMY KATZENELLENBOGEN: First of all, it made me somebody who has the foundations for making things happen. I was a very, very spoiled kid, and the military sort of put me on track and gave me the foundations, gave me the personality traits of a doer, I think. Maybe *doer* isn't the right word, but somebody who can . . .

JAMES: It taught you hard work.

TOMMY: Yeah, yeah. Now I know that if you want something, you can achieve it, and there's a process of doing it. That's probably the best thing that I got from the military.

JAMES: What do you mean by "there's a process of doing it"? Do you mean like a systematic process? Do you mean a psychological process?

TOMMY: I think it's more of a psychological process. I see a lot of people, so I mentor a lot of entrepreneurs and people. People today sort of expect things to happen to them. You say, "I want to have a company. I want to start up a company. I'll raise money and then I'll make a lot of money out of building a product and then I'm going to launch it and people are going to buy it." You can see that the way they're describing it, it's in a very passive way that things are happening. "People will buy my product." It's not that I'm going to sell them. They're going to buy my product. People are going to invest in me. It's not that I'm going to look for investments and I'm going to convince people. There is this notion.

I think the planning side of it—you know, the hardships, the contingencies, dealing with failure, expecting failure, learning from failure—these are things that I would say are the psychological mechanics of success. Nobody is born where everything just happens to them. I'm sure there are people like that, but that's one in a billion. Other than that, the rest of us, we really need to work hard in a systematic way of doing it.

JAMES: You learned, basically, the psychological side of hard work, systems, of getting things done. What's another lesson you learned from the military?

TOMMY: People. People skills, leadership skills, what it really is to be a leader, what it really is to be a manager, what's the difference between them. And the value of the team and the people behind you. No one can do things alone today. It's impossible. Getting the right team, what it takes to have the right team, what it means to have the right team, how to work with the team—these are the things that I think the military is very strong in.

Tommy's evolution, in education, in profession and, more importantly, personally is directly related to his service in the military. Tommy's forced break crucible helped him to develop his self-awareness, integrity, compassion and relatableness. Some of this growth is attributed to maturing, but the rigor and focus of his military experience drove his personal development.

Joe De Sena, CEO of Spartan Races and Burpee Master (Episode 58)

Joe is known to do burpees just about anywhere on the planet and at any time. I have seen a video of Joe going on a burpee spree at an airport. Then there was the time Joe decided to walk around with a 50-pound weight vest to test his limits. This guy is serious about stretching his personal limits and loves to test himself. However, Joe's biggest education about people came at 12 years old, when he started a pool-cleaning business in Queens, New York. His clients cut across society, including the mob. Joe describes why it was so great:

JOE DE SENA: Because they're very savvy people and you learn a lot from them. I wouldn't trade it in for the world. If you don't go down that road and get into trouble, the amount you can learn from it is fantastic. They're constantly... they're hustlers, right? They're constantly crafting up angles... I just love studying people. I had seven hundred customers in that business. I had customers that were Italian, I had customers that were black, that were Jewish, that were Irish. You name it—from everywhere. I had husbands that cheated on wives, wives that cheated on husbands, divorcees, people that went broke, people that became really successful, kids that grew up well, kids that went off the rails and got into drugs, kids that went to jail—and it was almost like this giant experiment for me looking through a fishbowl on the family I wanted to create and the things I didn't want to recreate. You can learn from it. You don't have to follow it.

JAMES: I think what is great about that though is what you just described is a way... You basically learn human nature across a variety of different verticals, so to speak: nationalities, colors, races, creeds, makeups, family makeups, whatever. You learn to read people by meeting so many different people.

JOE: Yeah.

Some of our most formative years are our early teens, and Joe's bizarro crucible of interacting with a cross-section of humans served him well. He learned how to read a situation, interact with individuals from different backgrounds and, as he says, work the angles. His world as a youth was a giant fishbowl, and he saw early on what he wanted to create and what he didn't want to create. For Joe and leaders like Joe, that translates into not giving up on an idea that they believe in. Further, Joe's example demonstrates how learning about others impacted his ability to relate to individuals across many walks of life. Take a minute and go to YouTube and find a video in which Joe talks about Spartan races. His passion for expanding them around the world is evident.

What Do These and Many Other Authentic Leaders Have in Common?

Joe, Tommy and Joe, and many other authentic leaders, use their crucible(s) as point of reflection and growth. (Are you sick of hearing about the crucible?) Like the three cases described above, the theme in my interviews was consistent in that *Crucible = Increased Self-Awareness.* Joe Friel discovered that his passion for understanding human performance and aging attracted a huge audience. Tommy, who initially resisted mandated military service, used the military, once he accepted his *forced pause* moment, to teach him how to succeed. Finally, Joe De Sena is Joe De Sena. If you haven't seen the video of him doing burpees in the airport, then you have missed something special. Joe used his experience of meeting others, watching them and learning how different individuals from different walks of life communicate and act. He also has this insatiable desire to test his body and his mind to learn more about himself.

All three are successful by all accounts, all three are motivated to be great people, and all three learned most from their crucible.

My Learning Journey: Perception Is Only That—Perception

I spent twenty years getting an education. One undergraduate degree, two master's degrees and a PhD, and I can say that I really never loved academic learning. I found it boring and uninspiring, and at times I was left thinking, "What's the point?"

I was also not good at school because I never learned how to study, focus and prepare for the way learning was structured and delivered. The concept was foreign to me, as it is for so many people who were taught by rote learning to memorize and ingest and throw that back up for a test. I always admired those who took to academic learning and excelled. I am sure that on some level this sounds like nonsense because I have had academic success, but perception tells only half the story. I graduated high school with a 2.5 GPA, but I played water polo and that was my ticket to get a conditional acceptance to university.

I graduated university with a 2.4 GPA (although I was a better student in my senior year—read "justification"), but I got into an MBA program because I was going to help coach a collegiate water polo team. I got into a PhD program for what I see as two specific reasons: one, the school did not require the Graduate Record Examinations (I am awful at standardized tests) and, two, I got a 3.4 GPA for my MBA. Oh, and remember from chapter 1—I called the administration every week for about twelve weeks. I was pleasant in my persistence, of course.

It wasn't until I began to pursue my PhD that I began to appreciate the process of learning, and I really enjoyed the topics and thinking of ways to solve practical business problems. At every step in my academic career, there were individuals who snickered behind my back, and who doubted my ability, work ethic and desire. I recognize that I'm not, academically, the sharpest tool in the shed, but what I have is resilience, or as Dr. Angela Duckworth calls it, grit.[5]

Where learning has had the largest impact in my development is in my personal growth. Moments of solitude provided great opportunities for learning, and luckily enough for me, I had plenty of opportunities to develop. I previously noted that I grew up in a family environment that was not as damaging as some of those you have read about in this book. Just listen to my Bridgette Mayer or Connie Pheiff interviews if you want to feel a bit better about your upbringing. But I was the youngest of three and a half (I had a stepbrother move into our house for his high school years) by five years—meaning, I was essentially an only child with the mentality of a youngest child. My mom and dad were not into the entertaining business, so I was often told to go use my imagination. As a parent of four, I can appreciate that now, as I learned to be in my own head—a lot—and to be self-sufficient. Self-sufficiency was also created from being a latchkey kid by third grade.

Early personal experiences were the catalyst for my personal journey to developing self-awareness. For me, self-awareness is a lifelong journey of learning, through reading, listening and paying attention to my crucibles: witnessing someone dying in a car wreck when I was 18, getting fired from my second job, getting a DUI and having to go to an outpatient rehabilitation program, moving to multiple countries and the death of my father. These moments provided critical opportunities for growth. Each one of my bizarro, forced break or avalanche crucibles allowed me to learn and develop my self-awareness, integrity, compassion and relatableness. However, it is my opinion that this happened only because, at least for personal development, I have a growth mindset.

Final Thoughts (for Now) on Learning

Many leaders interviewed for this book attribute their success to curiosity. It was their curiosity that drove them to learn more about themselves, their colleagues and their career choices. As I noted in chapter 2, I asked leaders what advice they would give their twenty-something self. I have no scientific evidence to support the following claim that I make, but to me it passes the sniff test:

Leaders who were able to articulate specific advice they would give themselves were orientated towards a growth mindset compared with those who appeared to have difficulties articulating advice. It is from the growth mindset that authentic leaders are born, because they have the willingness to receive hard truths, ask hard questions and get the best out of themselves. This in turn gets the best out of their colleagues across the organization.

When reviewing the transcripts, it became evident to me that an overwhelming number of authentic leaders used their crucible as a launching point for turning inward to gain a better understanding of who they are, what tools they needed personally and professionally, and where the path to growth lies. During my interview with Mo Gawdat (see chapter 1), we discussed how crucibles motivate leaders to develop personally and professionally. Here are some additional thoughts from Mo on the role crucibles play:

I wish we didn't have to [go through crucibles]. I sort of discussed that a little bit in the chapter about fear [in *Solve for Happy*], and I talked about how life tends to bring you face to face with your fears unless you decide to face them yourself. If you decide to take an initiative and develop without having to be pushed to develop, right, why go through the test?... If there is a skill you need to develop and you're not developing it, a little bit of harshness will have to push you to develop it. I call that *the nudge* in my book. (Episode 104)

Whether a leader is growth or fixed mindset oriented, life will eventually kick them in the face to deal with a crucible. Authentic leaders ride their crucible like a sideshow pony. (I admit, I don't know what that means, but someone once said it to me and it made me laugh.)

Dr. Randall Bell is known as the "Master of Disaster" due to his career choice. Randall is an economist who investigates disasters like 9-11, Chernobyl, Sandy Hook and more, to evaluate the economic loss for his clients. He typically arrives shortly after the event and sees all the carnage. Essentially, he goes into every human's worse nightmare situation. During our interview (episode 100), I asked him what attributes irritate him about his colleagues. He replied, "I think a lack of teachability... arrogance. I think that arrogance shuts down the growth potential in a person and I think [shuts down] just being teachable." I bring this up because Dr. Bell, like many other authentic leaders, sees the importance of learning both in their own development and in the development of their colleagues and the organization.

Finally, learning supports the overall Authentic Leadership Model and is at the core of the leaders who embrace the concept of authenticity. They use their growth mindset to be better leaders, always striving to learn more about themselves and develop their self-awareness.

Do You Practice a Growth Mindset?

Everyone has aspects of themselves that are growth mindset and fixed mindset focused. The difficulty for leaders arises when a fixed mindset falls in their blind spot. Carol Dweck provides a number of strategies to develop a growth mindset. These suggestions have an overarching aim to open a mindset to higher self-awareness, more compassion, clearer integrity and a heightened drive to be relatable.

1. *Track your success.* At the end of each week, take time to write down all your successes, no matter how big or how small. For example, you might have won a big client, worked out a number of times or simply given someone your undivided attention. Acknowledging your success allows you to appreciate the journey, again, no matter how big or how small.

2. *Study your failures.* Now that you have taken time to celebrate your successes, it is important to gain insight into your failures. No need to nitpick *all* failures during the week—that's counterproductive. Select one or two that are fresh in your mind and list all the reasons for them. Be careful not to list justifications, but honest reasons as to why a failure happened. Typically, justifications place blame on someone or something for the failure.

3. *Reflect on your goals.* Take time to reflect on your goals. Often goals are written down and tucked away somewhere to be forgotten. Instead, go back to your set goals, investigate, reflect on them and ask yourself, "What do I need to do to stay on track?" There is something very empowering about accomplishing a set goal.

4. *Confront the problem.* Think of something you need to do or a problem you want to confront. This can be personal or professional, but take time to make a conscious plan to follow. The more details the better, the more steps the better. Be vivid in your description.[6]

SIDENOTE: I often write goals as if I've completed them. For example, when I was 33 I wrote, "I wrote a book by the time I was 43." I will be 43 when this book is published. By writing a goal as if you have completed it, you create a subconscious marker in your brain. To be fair, I believe I looked at this goal only one other time, in my late thirties. But the goal stuck in my brain, and here you are.

Where Do We Go from Here? We Finish!

We have made it to the final ingredient that impacts a leader's ability to grow and develop. Learning is the overarching attribute that really drives a leader to develop their true self in the workplace. It is curiosity about all things that allows a leader to use their crucible as a tool for development and not as an excuse of defeat. And so, based on the additional variable, the authentic leadership equation has one final adaptation:

$$\text{Learning } [(\text{Crucible} = \Delta SA + (\Delta I + \Delta C + \Delta R))]\infty = \text{Authentic Leadership}$$

Wait, one small mention here: do you notice the infinity sign outside the last bracket? It's important to signify that the perspective one gains from the proposed formula never ends. You always go back to the beginning and repeat. And again, and again, because committing to authentic leadership requires work and time and energy and the desire to pull apart assumptions and beliefs—to inspect what is known and unknown and, most importantly, ask the meaningful question. It was Maslow who indicated that human beings, when all basic needs are met, strive for self-actualization.

The final chapter will take the equation and use one final story to sharpen the focus of how the Authentic Leadership Model can be explained. I'll attempt to tie up any loose ends that may exist and answer any possible questions. Grab your final beverage of choice, and practice your behavioral integrity by finishing what you started.

CONCLUSION

CLEARING THE PATH TO
AUTHENTIC LEADERSHIP

---

*I had to act like I knew everything. Everybody already
knows that you don't. I became very defensive. I didn't take
feedback very well. Finally, one of my bosses helped
me get over that. He said, "Lee, you don't need to know
everything. The whole world doesn't revolve around Lee,
so don't get so upset when I talk to you about things."
He helped me out with that.*

LEE COCKERELL (Episode 115)

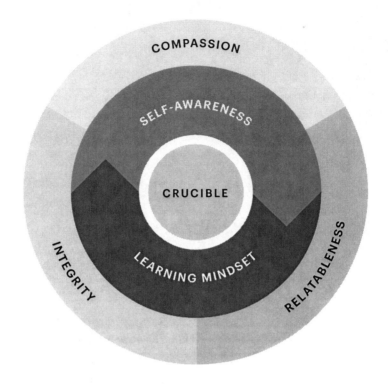

One Last Story

I introduced Lee Cockerell in chapter 4, on compassion. Lee's journey is like that of many of the other leaders I interviewed: his early life was his crucible. He was adopted twice as a kid, given the family name Cockerell as a teenager, and survived his time in the army. He never graduated from college. Although the odds were against him, Lee kept learning, kept working hard and kept dealing with his demons. I'll let Lee share a little of his story:

JAMES: I'm doing some research on you before we talked and I saw one of the videos in which you discuss one of the traits that you learned, which is "I can't do it all well, so I hire the people around me who can." Right? When did you discover that's the smarter way to go?

LEE COCKERELL: Well, I didn't know that when I was young. I was very insecure. Obviously, the way I grew up, I was adopted twice after my mother married five times and got my name, Cockerell, when I was 16. I didn't have a college degree. I was pretty insecure, a young guy. I had to act like I knew everything. Everybody already knows that you don't. I became very defensive. I didn't take feedback very well. Finally, one of my bosses helped me get over that. He said, "Lee, you don't need to know everything. The whole world doesn't revolve around Lee, so don't get so upset when I talk to you about things." He helped me out with that.

What I do is manage experts. You've got to let them do their thing. You've got to hire great ones. You can't hire idiots. The [good hires] do a great job. When you do that, you've got to figure out where you're going to spend your time if you're not an expert in those places. I did. I spent my time making sure we were hiring the right people.

I was involved in those systems, making sure I was involved in training, and also being a good role model for the culture of treating people right. That was my forte, and I pushed it hard. When I did it, all my people under me did it and it went all the way down. Role modeling is probably the best way people learn, including your kids at home.

JAMES: Can I ask you a question, because you said something earlier that really piqued my interest, and you can pass on this if you want to, but you mentioned that your mom was married five times and then you were adopted by, I'm assuming, two of her husbands throughout that process.

LEE: Yeah.

JAMES: Do you think that was the biggest, I guess, impact on you in terms of trust and personal growth? Do you think it stunted you in some ways...?

LEE: Oh, absolutely. I didn't trust anybody. I still have that little problem. It's down there.

JAMES: It would make sense.

LEE: Yeah. It's down there and it can come out, but I've learned to control it and to let it go. My wife said recently, "Lee, you don't aggravate me anymore." "Why?" I asked. "Because I decided to let it go [being right, insecure, etc.]." It's like that song from *Frozen*, "Let It Go." I had to get over that because it's in you. By the time you're 12, 13, 14, whatever you are, it's in you, emotionally. Yeah. I've learned to control it. I've learned to be more outgoing. I learned to be less defensive because I know people don't want to work with defensive people.

JAMES: How do you learn that, though? How do you unpack that for yourself and say, "Hey, listen, everyone out there is not trying to screw me."

LEE: Yeah. Well, I had a problem with one of my people at Marriott. I went out to see him and he had been transported to the hospital. He was so scared of me coming that he had dizziness and they checked him out. He came back. We had dinner and he told me that the way I got things done in those days was intimidating. I abused my authority and pushed people around.

After he told me that, I really came to grips with it. I thought about my grandmother, my mother. They'd kill me if they knew I was behaving that way. I started attending leadership courses. I went for a three-day course. I started reading about leaders that don't have authority and how they work. It took me a long time to get over it, but slowly and surely, I had more success and I learned to hire great people. As my success got better, my self-confidence got better.

I would say, today, my self-confidence is really big but there's still some [insecurities] down there, lurking . . . (Episode 115)

Back to Basics

The journey is coming to a close, and as you've made it this far, I want to say thank you, and I hope on some level the stories from our authentic leaders and the concept of being more authentic have resonated with you. Over the last six chapters, we have discussed self-awareness, integrity, compassion and relatableness—the need to create shared meaning, and that the authentic leader grows from their crucible. Growth is not enough, because it is also recognizing the opportunity to practice these leadership skills.

Karissa Thacker, Bill George and several other prominent leadership academics have worked to define authentic leadership, and in those definitions exist similarities about what it means to be and act as an authentic leader. Over the 140-plus interviews that inform this book, several similarities and macro themes emerge. Authentic leaders have the desire and ability to be true to themselves and true to others, and they maintain this authenticity across time and space. Recall our discussion of the 15 percent rule. Do you apply it?

Take a moment and reflect on these questions:

- Do you see yourself as an authentic leader?
- Can you give yourself honest critical feedback?
- Do you accept critical feedback from those around you?
- Do you broadcast your team's successes and your failures?
- Can you motivate those around you with shared experiences?
- Are you compassionate and keen to relieve your colleagues' suffering, whether it's coffee during a moment of anxiety or comforting someone over a death in the family?
- Do you live your life with integrity—not only moral integrity but behavioral integrity? Do you apply the rule "Do unto others as you would have them do unto you?" Do you ask yourself, "How would I want my kids to see me act?"

- Do you go out of your way to create shared experiences? Do you want people to have interactions with you that they can remember, no matter how big and small?
- Are you driven to learn? Are you driven to understand other people better? Are you driven to educate yourself in your profession? Do you go to seminars? Do you take extra classes?
- What motivates and drives you? Is it pure of heart, or Machiavellian?

Throughout this book I discuss the importance of crucibles for an authentic leader's growth. The crucible is a central theme in a leader's development. But the crucible is impactful only for those leaders who are willing to embrace it. Otherwise, the crucible will be damaging and remain a negative event that *prevents* acceptance, learning and growth. It's when you choose to let go of that event and embrace it from the standpoint of growth that the crucible becomes that amazing jumping-off point for self-discovery and self-awareness.

Authentic leaders who embrace a growth mindset understand that life is a journey and that the train they are on is not about the destination, but rather about the exploration. Thus, the cycle of crucible, self-awareness and learning is essential for growth of compassion, integrity and relatableness.

Moving Forward with the Authentic Leadership Model (ALM)

We're all on a journey in life. Who we are today is not who we're going to be tomorrow, and eventually that journey ends. We all die at some point. Many leaders I interviewed had experienced the loss of a parent or sibling. For me, that moment was at age 20, and it led to asking this question: "Am I a better version of myself this year than last?" I hope that as you read the stories of these authentic leaders, you are inspired to ask the same question.

The model was developed as an easy visual tool to help you reflect on the basic human factors that inform your authentic leadership journey. It can also be used to help HR, executives and coaches take a systematic approach to how an individual's professional crucible is impeding their growth. For example, perhaps a team lead is struggling to manage their team. By utilizing the ALM, you can help the individual articulate that a previous supervisor led by intimidation and fear. You can take this professional crucible and begin to create strategies or get resources to help the team lead manage with more clarity.

Being an Authentic Leader Is Hard

Being authentic is hard! You have to be open, embrace fear of being judged, hold true to your beliefs and take strength from your confidence. And you need to be inspiring, patient and compassionate. As I said in the introduction, being an authentic leader is a constant work in progress. Malcolm Gladwell, in his book *Outliers*, suggests that true experts dedicate on average 10,000 hours of work towards their skill.[1] I like to ponder that if we spent as much time on our authentic self as Bill Gates, Michael Jordan or Oprah Winfrey did at their careers, what would be the result? Well, Oprah made a living doing that, but still, you get the point.

We all have insecurities and shortcomings, and we are all fallible. It is what it is, and we're uncomfortable when our limitations are revealed to people we do not know intimately. Our underbelly, when exposed, can be seen as ugly. Take a minute and think of a leader who owns their underbelly—their shortcomings and their limitations—and hires the individuals around them to make up for the shortcomings. How might you relate to that leader? How do they perform? What are interactions like? Respectful? Meaningful?

It is my opinion, and will remain so until I am convinced otherwise, that authentic leadership is the 21st-century type of leadership that will propel underperforming organizations to outperform the competition. With Generations Y and Z moving into management over the next five to twenty years, organizations will be dealing with groups that have fully embraced social media. With social media comes the blurring of the professional and private self, and whether intentional or not, this will blur the line between professional and personal life. This blurring of the line will shine a light on those who are inauthentic. As has been a theme in this book, authenticity leads to trust, loyalty and engagement.

Final Thoughts—I Promise

When you become more self-aware and put more effort into learning and into engaging with the world to become a "better you," you come to realize that acts of compassion and living with integrity offer a high return on investment. When you take time to listen to those around you, ask more questions and be slow with your own answers, you will make true connections with people and create moments brimming with meaning. These moments can come in the form of a small exchange over a coffee, a walk together or a hug, but the point is, it's in the sharing, and more importantly what it means for the person.

Change is hard, change is difficult and change is all about choice. Changing one's behavior and thought process is not easy. It will be uncomfortable, inconvenient and at times overwhelming. And you know what? That's awesome, because it means you're trying. With consistent effort and focus will come rewards, so I encourage you as you go through this process of becoming a more authentic leader to ask the hard questions and apply the steps at the end of each chapter. You might want to seek out a mentor or a business or lifestyle coach. Find somebody who's willing to keep you accountable. What you will discover in life is that as well-intentioned as our desired change is, it's hard to make it happen unless you have someone keeping you accountable, holding your feet to the fire and making you answer for your successes and your failures.

Be Your Own Velveteen Rabbit

After my DUI, I spent the six months in an outpatient program, learning a lot. At one point the counselor wanted to make a point of self-love and that accepting yourself for who you are is an important part of growth. To make this point, she read an excerpt from the beloved children's book *The Velveteen Rabbit*, by Margery Williams. It was one of the most powerful experiences in the entire program, so I want to leave with this:

"What is REAL?" asked the Rabbit one day, when they were lying side by side near the nursery fender, before Nana came to tidy the room. "Does it mean having things that buzz inside you and a stick-out handle?"

"Real isn't how you are made," said the Skin Horse. "It's a thing that happens to you. When a child loves you for a long, long time, not just to play with, but REALLY loves you, then you become Real."

"Does it hurt?" asked the Rabbit.

"Sometimes," said the Skin Horse, for he was always truthful. "When you are Real you don't mind being hurt."

"Does it happen all at once, like being wound up," he asked, "or bit by bit?"

"It doesn't happen all at once," said the Skin Horse. "You become. It takes a long time. That's why it doesn't happen often to people who break easily, or have sharp edges, or who have to be carefully kept. Generally, by the time you are Real, most of your hair has been loved off, and your eyes drop out and you get loose in the joints and very shabby. But these things don't matter at all, because once you are Real you can't be ugly, except to people who don't understand."[2]

. . .

"Don't let fear conquer you. Conquer your fears and become your own authentic leader."

DR. JAMES KELLEY
Authentic Leadership Expert

ACKNOWLEDGMENTS

THE LIST OF those who have impacted me on this journey is wide and the trail is long. To all of you who nudged me over time, I say thank you.

I would like in particular to thank my mom, Alice Kelley. When I was 9 years old, a friend and I would chant in response to my mom's ability to talk, "Alice, O Alice, get off the phone, because if you don't, we will burn down your home." Thank you for being a stable consistent force that has never wavered in support of my nomad ways. To Linda Guzman: without your home in the summers, I am not sure what trouble I would have gotten into. You were always willing to feed me, entertain me and teach me about compassion, integrity and pursuit of happiness. To Mary: you are my rock and muse for being a better person. I fall short on many occasions, but with you by my side, I will work to be a better person. To Branson, Lucy, Miles and Isla: you are my world, and every choice I make is with you four in my mind. To the entirety of the above mentioned, your impact is immeasurable.

This book is dedicated to my dad, who passed away when I was 20 years old. I don't know how life would have been different with him in it, but I surely know how his being gone has impacted me. His death is a ripple in my life that continues to create waves twenty years later, and I am grateful for that.

I would also like to thank the United Arab Emirates University for financial support. Thank you, Page Two Strategies. The support you provided to a newbie author was comforting, and confidence building. Your organization is top notch. Finally, I want to thank Don Looney, the editor who instilled confidence when I needed it most. You are a legend.

NOTES

Introduction: The Importance of Being Genuine

1. Amy Adkins, "Employee Engagement Survey," *Gallup News* (13 January 2016), www.gallup.com/poll/188144/employee-engagement-stagnant-2015.aspx.

2. World Health Organization and World Bank, "Investing in treatment for depression and anxiety leads to fourfold return," news release (13 April 2016), www.who.int/mediacentre/news/releases/2016/depression-anxiety-treatment/en/.

3. Jessica Grossmeier, Ray Fabius, Jennifer P. Flynn, Steven P. Noeldner, Dan Fabius, Ron Z. Goetzel & David R. Anderson, "Linking workplace health promotion best practices and organizational financial performance: Tracking market performance of companies with highest scores on the HERO scorecard," *Journal of Occupational and Environmental Medicine* 58, no. 1 (2016): 16–23.

4. Andrew J. Oswald, Eugenio Proto & Daniel Sgroi, *Happiness and Productivity* (10 February 2014), www2.warwick.ac.uk/fac/soc/economics/staff/academic/proto/workingpapers/happinessproductivity.pdf.

Chapter 1: The Crucible

1. Warren Bennis, *On Becoming a Leader* (New York: Knopf, 1989; 2nd edition, 2009).

2. Warren Bennis & Robert J. Thomas, "Crucibles of Leadership," *Harvard Business Review* (September 2002).

Chapter 2: Self-Awareness

1. Jane Turner & Sharon Mavin, "Becoming more self aware—A journey of authentic leader development," 15th International Conference on Human Resource Development Research and Practice across Europe, 4–6 June 2014, Edinburgh, U.K.
2. Brené Brown, *The Gifts of Imperfection: Let Go of Who You Think You're Supposed to Be and Embrace Who You Are* (Center City, MN: Hazelden Publishing, 2010), p. 125.
3. Joe Burton, *Creating Mindful Leaders* (New York: Wiley, 2018).

Chapter 3: Integrity

1. Daniel E. Palmer, "Business leadership: Three levels of ethical analysis," *Journal of Business Ethics* 88, no. 3 (September 2009): 525–36.
2. William L. Gardner, Bruce J. Avolio, Fred Luthans, Douglas R. May & Fred Walumbwa, " 'Can you see the real me?' A self-based model of authentic leader and follower development." *The Leadership Quarterly* 16, no. 3 (2005): 343–72.
3. Fred Kiel, *Return on Character: The Real Reason Leaders and Their Companies Win* (Cambridge, MA: Harvard Business Review Press, 2015).
4. Sam Harris, *Lying* (Four Elephants Press, 2013).
5. Tony Simons, "Behavioral integrity: The perceived alignment between managers' words and deeds as a research focus," *Organization Science* 13, no. 1 (2002): 18–35.
6. Tony Simons, "What message does your conduct send? Building integrity to boost your leadership effectiveness," *Cornell Hospitality Report* 14, no. 24 (2014): 6–10.
7. Karissa Thacker, *The Art of Authenticity: Tools to Become an Authentic Leader and Your Best Self* (Hoboken, NJ: John Wiley & Sons, 2016).
8. Bill George, *Authentic Leadership: Rediscovering the Secrets to Creating Lasting Value* (San Francisco: Jossey-Bass, 2004).

Chapter 4: Compassion

1. The Dalai Lama & Nicholas Vreeland, *An Open Heart: Practicing Compassion in Everyday Life* (New York: Little, Brown and Company, 2001), p. 8.
2. Stephen S. Hall, *Wisdom: From Philosophy to Neuroscience* (New York: Vintage, 2011).
3. Monica Worline & Jane Dutton, *Awakening Compassion at Work: The Quiet Power That Elevates People and Organizations* (New York: Berrett-Koehler Publishers, 2017).

4. Karen A. Armstrong, *The Great Transformation: The Beginning of Our Religious Traditions* (New York: Anchor Books, 2006).

5. Kim S. Cameron, David Bright & Arran Caza, "Exploring the relationships between organizational virtuousness and performance," *American Behavioral Scientist* 47, no. 6 (2004): 766–90.

6. Leonardo Badea & Nicolae Alexandru Pan, "The role of empathy in developing the leader's emotional intelligence," *Theoretical & Applied Economics* 17, no. 2 (2010): 69–78.

7. Elizabeth Pybus, *Human Goodness: Generosity and Courage* (Toronto: University of Toronto Press, 1991), p. 59.

Chapter 5: Relatableness

1. Daniel H. Pink, *Drive: The Surprising Truth about What Motivates Us* (New York: Penguin, 2011).

2. Edward L. Deci & Richard M. Ryan, "The empirical exploration of intrinsic motivational processes," pp. 39–80 in L. Berkowitz (ed.), *Advances in Experimental Social Psychology*, vol. 13 (New York: Academic Press, 1980).

3. Amy Adkins, "Employee engagement stagnant in 2015," *Gallup News* (13 January 2016), www.gallup.com/poll/188144/employee-engagement-stagnant-2015.aspx.

4. Arlen C. Moller, Edward L. Deci & Andrew J. Elliot, "Person-level relatedness and the incremental value of relating," *Personality and Social Psychology Bulletin* 36, no. 6 (2010): 754–67.

5. Tim Minchin, University of Western Australia 2013 Commencement Speech, www.youtube.com/watch?v=yoEezzD71sc.

6. Michael Maccoby, "Narcissistic leaders: The incredible pros, the inevitable cons," *Harvard Business Review* 78, no. 1 (2000): 68–78.

7. Dale Carnegie, *How to Win Friends and Influence People*, 3rd ed. (New York: Random House, 1981).

Chapter 6: Learning

1. Carol S. Dweck, *Mindset: The New Psychology of Success* (New York: Random House, 2006).

2. Mary C. Murphy & Carol S. Dweck, "Mindsets shape consumer behavior," *Journal of Consumer Psychology* 26, no. 1 (2016): 127–36.

3. Angel Duckworth, *Grit: The Power of Passion and Perseverance* (New York: Simon & Schuster, 2016).

Conclusion: Clearing the Path to Authentic Leadership

1. Malcolm Gladwell, *Outliers: The Story of Success* (New York: Little, Brown, 2008).

2. Margery Williams, *The Velveteen Rabbit*, with illustrations by William Nicholson (New York: George H. Doran, 1922).

FURTHER READING

Amanuel G. Tekleab, Henry P. Sims Jr., Seokhwa Yun, Paul E. Tesluk & Jonathan Cox, "Are we on the same page? Effects of self-awareness of empowering and transformational leadership," *Journal of Leadership & Organizational Studies* 14, no. 3 (2008): 185-201.

Anthony Gatling, Patricia A. Castelli, & Matthew Lawrence Cole, "Authentic leadership: The role of self-awareness in promoting coaching effectiveness," *Asia-Pacific Journal of Management Research and Innovation* 9, no. 4 (2013): 337-347.

LEADERSHIP PERSPECTIVES

1. Joe Burton, CEO of Whil Concepts
2. Lisa McDonald, host of Living Fearlessly
3. Jay Scott, co-director of Alex's Lemonade Stand Foundation
4. Elise Carr, MA, sexuality expert
5. Brad Stulberg, co-author of *Peak Performance: Elevate Your Game, Avoid Burnout, and Thrive with the New Science of Success*
6. Daniele Giovannucci, president and CEO of the Committee on Sustainability and Assessment.
7. The Very Reverend Richard Pengelley, dean of Perth's Anglican Diocese
8. Mo Gawdat, chief business officer of Google X
9. Bridgette Mayer, owner of Bridgette Mayer Art Gallery
10. Doug Smith, CEO of Doug Smith Performance & second pick overall in the 1981 NHL hockey draft
11. Dennis Boyle, co-founder and partner at IDEO
12. James Poer, CEO of Kestra Financial
13. Lisa Buckingham, chief human resources officer for Lincoln Financial
14. Greg Justice, CEO of National Corporate Fitness Institute
15. Mark Crowley, leadership expert and former senior vice president of sales leadership at Washington Mutual
16. Chris Boyce, founder and vice chairman at Virgin Pulse
17. Ron Wiens, president of Ron Wiens Consulting
18. Dr. Seth Gillihan, practicing psychologist
19. Dr. Kara O'Leary, practicing psychologist
20. Larry Chapman, CEO of the Chapman Institute
21. Joe De Sena, CEO of Spartan Races

22. Dr. John Nagl, a retired colonel and headmaster at the Haverford School for Boys
23. Brad Cooper, CEO of U.S. Corporate Wellness
24. Jeffrey Hayzlett, chairman of C-Suite Networks
25. Jennifer Benz, CEO of Benz Communication
26. Lee Cockerell, former executive vice president of operations for Walt Disney World Resort
27. Laura Putnam, CEO of Motion Infusion and bestselling author of *Workplace Wellness That Works*
28. Dr. Joel Bennett, CEO of Organizational Wellness & Learning Systems
29. Greg Zlevor, founder & CEO of Westwood International
30. Mitch Martens, the employee wellness administrator at Cedars-Sinai Medical Center
31. Dr. Michelle Robin, chief wellness officer and founder of The Wellness Connection
32. Dr. Richard Ryan, professor at Australian National University & University of Rochester
33. Connie Pheiff, a former CEO of Girl Scouts and currently an entrepreneur and podcast host
34. Sean Geehan, CEO of Geehan Group
35. Andrew Schirmer, president of McCann Global Health
36. Joe Friel, legendary triathlon coach, innovator and really nice guy
37. Tommy Katzenellenbogen, chief strategy officer at Cron Systems

ABOUT THE AUTHOR

Author, speaker and consultant DR. JAMES KELLEY was born in Portland, Oregon. Following the completion of an MBA and a year of teaching English in Japan, Kelley moved to Australia to pursue his PhD in International Marketing. He is the host of the *Executives After Hours* podcast, where he states, "I care about who you are, not what you do, because who you are defines what you do." Kelley currently teaches at United Arab Emirates University, and resides near Dubai with his wife, Mary, and their four children.

www.drjameskelley.com

CPSIA information can be obtained
at www.ICGtesting.com
Printed in the USA
FFOW02n1712070418
46160174-47343FF

9 780999 891513